Princess Hayley

the jewish princess
feasts & festivals

Enjoy Everything

Lots of love

Georgie xxx

Tracey

the jewish princess
feasts &
festivals

Georgie Tarn & Tracey Fine

STERLING

New York / London
www.sterlingpublishing.com

STERLING and the distinctive Sterling logo are registered trademarks of
Sterling Publishing Co., Inc.

Library of Congress Cataloging-in-Publication Data Available

10 9 8 7 6 5 4 3 2 1

Published by Sterling Publishing Co., Inc.
387 Park Avenue South, New York, NY 10016
© 2009 Georgie Tarn & Tracey Fine
Illustrations © 2009 Karen Greenberg
Design and layout @ 2009 Quadrille Publishing Limited

Distributed in Canada by Sterling Publishing
c/o Canadian Manda Group, 165 Dufferin Street,
Toronto, Ontario, Canada M6K 3H6

Printed in Singapore by KHL Printing Co Pte Ltd

Sterling ISBN 978-1-4027-6923-8

For information about custom editions, special sales, premium and
corporate purchases, please contact Sterling Special Sales
Department at 800-805-5489 or specialsales@sterlingpublishing.com.

dedication

We dedicate this book to our Queen Mothers, who, like a great pair of jeans, keep getting better with age. (Who do you think taught us the meaning of "self-maintenance"?) They always give us advice, whether asked for or not. ("I don't want to interfere, but…") They are always at the end of the phone—wherever they happen to be! They go out of their way to make sure we have everything they never had—and give us everything they don't want. They know every ailment: Either they have heard of it, know someone who has had it, or they've had it themselves. They know every specialist for every ailment and make regular royal appointments.

We know you are very proud of us, because you tell the whole world. Keep it up: It's fabulous PR! Put this in your *naches* book!

contents

Acknowledgments   8
Introduction   12
   Mazel tov & Siman tov   13
   Let Me Present...   14

Festivals   16
   Purim   18
   Passover   28
   Shavuot   48
   Rosh Hashanah & Yom Kippur   62
   Succot   84
   Hanukkah   102

Celebrations   118
   The Bris Brunch   120
   The Bar Mitzvah   134
   The Wedding   152

Feasts   168
   Hosting the Designer Dinner Party   170
   A Collection of Canapés   174
   A Chicken Dinner Party   178
   A Fish Dinner Party   186
   Vegetarian Princess, Italian-style   194

Yiddish Expressionism   200
Index   206

acknowledgments

Well, we've done it. WE ARE AUTHORS! *The Jewish Princess Cookbook* is in print. It's extraordinary that, for Princesses who love new products (especially anti-wrinkle creams; we always live in hope of finding one that WORKS), we have created a product ourselves! We can go shopping for our own creation.

Not that we *do*...

Well, OK. So there are just a few copies hidden under the bed.

Yes, being stacked on shelves has become a shopping kick. We enter a bookshop and our pulses begin to race. We see *The Jewish Princess Cookbook* and our hearts start to pound. We hide behind bookcases to see if there are any Princess Pickers. When they appear (we're prepared to wait *hours*), our pink pens are ready to sign.

WE ARE OUR OWN STALKERS!

To be honest, this whole book thing came as a bit of a shock to our Princess Pals. They simply couldn't believe we had written a book. After all, whenever we mentioned the word "book," they immediately started suggesting restaurants. (Nowadays, of course, we are "booked" at all the trendiest fusions.) So we gave up and decided to keep it a secret.

Actually, we really enjoyed leading a Princess double life. If we were caught in town in Princess Power-suits (retro-*Dynasty*), we said, "Consultation," and our Princess Pals gave us that knowing look. When spotted buying copious amounts of food, we said, "Family." They looked sympathetic. When we had to fly to New York, yes, you guessed it: We said, "SHOPPING!"

We were immediately given a list.

Now they all know the big secret. We broke the news at a dinner party (you should have seen their faces). After the initial "WHY DIDN'T YOU TELL US?," they were all ultra-enthusiastic and began to nag us to get back on our thrones (well, we *are* JPs) and start typing *a new one*.

So we sat there, wondering whether we could do it again. Would we Princess Panic: be thrown into early literary menopause and need CF— Calf's Foot Jelly (a kosher savory delicacy)—to get our creative juices flowing? NEVER! We just remembered to be PPP:

*POSITIVE,

*PRODUCTIVE,

*And, of course, PRINCESSLIKE!

So here we are: again!

To reach the summit of success (first or second time) you need a lot of help. We have to say that our friends, family, colleagues, and even complete strangers (the couple on the airplane to Spain; you know who you are) came up trumps.

So a great big Honey Cake Hug to the following: our mothers, Helen Fine and Sandra Chester, for interior-designing bookstores globally, moving *The Jewish Princess Cookbook* to prime position; our fathers, Tony Fine and David Chester, still on the golf course (their handicaps haven't improved); in-laws Bobbie and Irvin Tarn, for cross-Atlantic advice (they have flown the coop to sunny Florida); and Birgitta Simone, Hayley Leslie, Lisa Tray, Vanessa Class, and Michelle Grossman, for doing the school-run when Princesses G & T are out at Princess Meetings.

Many thanks, too, to the following Princesses for their input: Louise Caplin, Katie Vincent, Sima Fine, Zilda Collins, Lynda Brown, Sonia Levy, Monica Slater, Gillian Marsden, Elaine Grant, Karen Tarn, Cindy Kariel, Karen Gerrard, Mandy Stanley, Roz Laren, Louise Harris, Joanne Kaye, Deborah Bright, Debbie Addler, Lisa Marks, Mandy and Amanda Chester, and Auntie Rosalind Chester.

And thank you to Rabbi Meir Salasnik for answering the Rabbi hotline with help and advice. Also to Victor Kramer (kosher texter); Andrew Thompson, our lawyer, who keeps getting us out of sticky situations; Tony and Richard from ABDA, our website designers: thank you, thank you!

Catherine in Harrods, who told us our book would be *huge*; Carolynne Wyper: a GEM! Then there's Anne-Marie, The Hairdresser, who drops everything for a JP crisis; Adam Lawrence, Royal Photographer; Dorie, our literary agent, who we still drive insane 24/7 and has become a great friend; Anne Kibel, our management agent (who we will drive mad): Welcome aboard; Nick Painter, Waitrose Wonderman; Karen Greenberg, our illustrator: a Princess in The Big Apple; Claire Peters, JP Stylist; Mark McGinlay, our PR Prince at Quadrille; David Segrue: We will sign for you any time, any place, anywhere; Jane O'Shea and all at Quadrille who make dreams come true; Jamie Ambrose, our lovely, understanding editor: Hope we didn't give you too much work this time around!

And, of course, our brothers, sisters, sisters-in-law, nieces, and nephews for tasting all our teatime treats; Caroline Sammuels: Whenever we meet, you offer a pearl of wisdom; Stephen Marks, for trying to explain VAT (Very Aggravating Tax!): We still don't get it; our children, Max, Channie, Cassie, Eden, and Darcy: culinary critics; Rat, Georgie's Prince Charming: Thank you for all your time, support (this isn't just financial!), and belief in The Jewish Princess project (he's hoping to retire...).

And finally, thank you to all our Princess fans from all over the world. We love you dearly and are sure you will see us hiding in your bookstore soon, pink pens at the ready.

What does a Jewish Princess write?

Checks!

mazel tov & siman tov
celebrate good times—come on!

I am now officially over my midlife crisis, but don't worry: I haven't had THE face-lift—*yet*. (It's amazing what a fabulous new haircut can do...) I have, however, come to an age when it's time to take stock, and this doesn't just mean chicken soup.

When I left my mother's womb—by Caesarean, of course—the first words I heard were *Mazel Tov*. I was bundled up, washed, weighed (the first of many times), fingers and toes counted, and then put into my very first new OUTFIT (again, the first of many!). *Lechayim* chimed around the room; the blessing means "To life," and was bestowed upon me so that I would *live*, therefore it was my Princess duty to carry this out to the FULL.

Unlike Forrest Gump, my life is *not* like a box of chocolates—even though I do, of course, have a special Princess Passion for chocolate. My life is a buffet: a metaphorical table that stretches out before me, crammed full with a cornucopia of flavors and experiences. There are so many choices that it's difficult to Princess Pick, but my advice is to try a *bissel* of everything. If there's a queue, you might even be inclined to push forward, but if you do, then you might also miss out on meeting that special person standing right by your side. However, when you reach the end of the buffet, are full to the brim, and cannot take another bite, the most important thing is that you'll know you have lived, loved, and ENJOYED.

So, speaking of enjoyment, there's no time to waste: Grab your Princess Plate, knives, forks, handbags—and shoes, of course. You are invited to join the queue at my buffet, to whine and dine at my table, to share my festivals and feasts with family and friends, and to hear some pearls of wisdom and gain some diamond advice along the way. Of course, you're also invited to try my delicious, new, and easy recipes for all these special occasions.

Yes, The Jewish Princess is back, with her hair and nails done, so it's time once again to INDULGE!

let me present...

Like all Princesses I love making a *shiddach* (a successful introduction), so here goes:

DO I HAVE SOME RECIPES FOR YOU!

There are certain foods you are introduced to in your life which have such a profound effect on you that, whenever you eat them, see them, or even sniff them, you are transported back to a time where you either bonded forever or were confounded that people could touch the stuff (a bit like blind dates).

I have to say that, with most dishes, one taste and I was hooked. However, a few foods still do produce Food Fear. It is odd, because as a child experiencing Jewish cuisine, I did eat some rather strange things. The chicken's foot, for example: You cannot find a stranger food, yet after it has been boiled in soup, sucking on such a foot (belonging only to a chicken, mind you) was and is an absolutely delicious experience, as was eating liver and even oxtail. Now, even though a chicken's foot definitely *looks* like a chicken's foot, I never had a problem with it, yet if you so much as mention TONGUE, I feel the shiver of Food Fear run down my back. No tongue sandwiches will be touching my tongue—and this is not said tongue-in-cheek (excuse the pun). From the first moment I saw tongue, complete with tastebuds, I knew I could never go there.

However, the Jewish Princess's calendar is filled with many other wonderful foods, and, just like the Jewish Princess's pantry, it is always full to the brim, what with all the holidays, celebrations, and the odd dinner-party feast thrown in. Hardly a month goes by without an excuse to make a special dish, whip up a favorite dessert, or smell the *yom tov* (holiday) cake baking in the oven. At certain times of the year I have a calling—and this isn't just when my fancy-dress outfit has arrived for Purim! This yearning makes me rekindle my love for certain dishes, and even though I could eat them all year round, I don't—a bit like wearing white jeans.

In April, I meet up and enjoy a spring fling with coconut macaroons and matzo *brie* during the eight days of Passover (see page 28).

Early summer sees me marching into the supermarket to celebrate Shavuot, picking up tubs and tubs of cream cheese to whisk up my JP favorite Mars Bar Cheesecake (page 60).

At the end of the summer I can't wait for my brief encounter with apples, dipping them into honey to honor a sweet Jewish New Year. After that, I keep slicing slivers of Honey Cake (page 81) until I have eaten the whole thing; even then I continue to bake more and keep slivering away until the end of Yom Kippur ten days later.

On Yom Kippur (the Day of Atonement,) I break my fast on foods that are salty but nice, such as anchovies and herring. While they are totally unsuitable after fasting and not drinking a drop of liquid for twenty-five hours (I always go to bed with serious heartburn), as long as they're accompanied by endless, thirst-quenching cups of tea—AND MORE HONEY CAKE—I know I've made it to another year!

Just when you thought the holidays were over, three more turn up: Succot (page 84), Shemini Atzeret, and, to finish off, Simchat Torah. This gives me just enough time to recover and then look forward to Princess Present Week, otherwise known as Hanukkah (page 102).

Of course, in between all the Jewish holidays there are so many other reasons to celebrate, from birthday parties (another JP favorite) to dinner parties and even the occasional wedding, bar or bat mitzvah, or *bris*. Before you know it, the year has come and gone in a wonderful festival of FOOD!

Yes, all the tastes of the year have a special place in my heart (please never try to feed me heart, though: I just couldn't) and being reintroduced to them again and again really does make each and every day special. So I have many treats in store for you within the following pages, and as you read, please ENJOY.

I hope that now that I have made a successful *shiddach*, you will be very happy indeed.

I

festivals

purim
the festival of lots

If ever a festival celebrated a Jewish Princess, Purim has to be it. This epic tale of blockbuster proportions really does prove that a Jewish Princess can change the course of history.

Now, you may never have thought of Queen Esther as a JP, but here is my evidence. First, although she was tragically orphaned as a child and brought up by her Uncle Mordecai, this did not stop her from getting ahead. With her Princess Positive attitude, she followed her uncle's advice, keeping *shtoom* that she was a JP (well, the king wouldn't want to know about her shopping habits) and entered the royal Persian beauty contest to replace the king's first wife, Vashti, with a younger, more beautiful model (some things never change). She took first place and the *shiddach* was made. Esther had gone from Jewish Princess to QUEEN.

I wonder if she got a bigger ring?

In her new life at court, she did not forget Mordecai—in fact, quite the opposite. When he came to her with news that Haman, the king's chief advisor, was plotting to murder the Jewish people, she knew she had to help. The lots* had literally been thrown (thus the festival of lots), and the date for the massacre set.

For three days Esther prepared at her peril to enter the king's inner court. To do this, she detoxed (fasted) and, I presume, had her hair and nails done. When the king saw her, she was welcomed (obviously she had a good hairdresser) and what did she do? She invited the king and Haman to dinner.

As any JP knows, the way to a man's heart is through his stomach.

---

*Lots was an actual game played by throwing stones.

Once the king and Haman had enjoyed her fabulous banquet (I bet she over-catered), Esther told the king of Haman's terrible plot and revealed that she was, in fact, a Jewish Princess. She didn't make a *megillah* (song and dance) about it, even though when we read the story of Purim, it is read from a scroll called a *megillah*. The king, like any man whose JP wife has given him a *misha bayruch* (telling off), realized he should do exactly what he was told. Therefore, justice was served: Haman was put to death and Mordecai, in true Jewish tradition, followed into the family business, becoming the king's chief advisor.

Every year this festival is celebrated in true JP style, and it is customary to get dressed up (not a Princess Problem), have parties, eat sweet triangular pastries known as *Hamantaschen* (representing the three corners of Haman's hat; see page 24), give gifts of chocolate and cake to friends and family (known as *mishloach manot*), and even to get a little *shiker*.

What better way to remember Queen Esther, an *Eshet Chayil*: a woman of worth, and a true Jewish Princess?

What did the Jewish Princess do for Purim?

She put on her new, fancy dress!

drunken fish

serves 4

1¾ cups vegetable stock
8 small, skinless sole or flounder
    fillets, about 5 ounces each
salt to taste
2 tablespoons Chinese
    cooking wine

1 fresh, red Thai chile (use less if
    you don't like it too spicy)
a few slices of grated fresh ginger
4 scallions, only the white
    part, cut horizontally
3 tablespoons chopped cilantro

In a large pan, bring the stock to a boil, then reduce the heat
so that it simmers.

Wash the sole and season with a little salt.

Add the Chinese cooking wine to the stock, along with the chile,
ginger, and scallions. Cook, stirring occasionally, for 1 minute.

Add the chopped cilantro and the fish to the stock mixture.
Continue simmering until the fish is cooked.

*Why not get dressed up Chinese-style (I love Shanghai Tang) and
serve this with rice and chopsticks?*

a shissel of shikerer chicken

serves 6

3–4 tablespoons olive oil
  (depending on the size
  of chicken)
2 onions, diced
1 large chicken, cut into 8 pieces
⅔ cup all-purpose flour
3 cups white wine

14-ounce can crushed tomatoes
2 cups boiled water
1 tablespoon vegetable
  bouillon powder
4-ounce jar of sliced black olives
1 teaspoon dried oregano
salt and black pepper to taste

Heat the oil in a frying pan and fry the onions until slightly browned. Transfer to a large *shissel*, or cooking pot.

Roll each piece of chicken in the flour, then fry in the olive oil until lightly browned. Place in the *shissel*.

Pour in the wine and let it cook for about 1 minute, then add the tomatoes, water, bouillon powder, olives, oregano, and salt and pepper to taste. Bring to a boil and simmer for 1 hour.

Remove the chicken from the *shissel* and turn up the heat. Cook briskly until you can see a difference in volume, 10–15 minutes. Stir constantly while the sauce reduces to ensure that it doesn't stick to the bottom of the pot and burn.

Preheat the oven to 350°F. Place the chicken in a baking dish and pour the thickened sauce over the top. Cover and cook in the oven for 15 minutes.

A tasty chicken dish, but make sure the children don't get shiker!

jerk burgers

makes approximately 16

2¼ pounds ground turkey
1 tablespoon jerk spice
1 extra-large egg
2 tablespoons matzo meal
vegetable oil for frying
16-ounce can sliced pineapple
   rings in their own juice

juice of 1½ limes
iceberg lettuce
16 small hamburger buns

Mix the first four jerk burger ingredients together. Moisten your hands with water, take a large tablespoon of the mixture, and form it into a patty. Repeat until you have 16.

Fry the patties until golden brown, 5–10 minutes on each side.

When ready to serve, put the pineapple rings and their juice in a large saucepan. Add the lime juice and heat through.

Drain away the juice, then place one pineapple ring under each burger and serve with the iceberg lettuce in the buns.

A burger to spice up your life.

prune and chocolate hamantaschen

makes approximately 40

for the filling
7 ounces dark chocolate
¾ cup soft pitted prunes
2 tablespoons sour cream
1 tablespoon brandy

for the pastry
1 cup (2 sticks) softened
  unsalted butter
scant ½ cup packed light
  brown sugar
2 extra-large egg yolks
2¾ cups all-purpose flour
1 teaspoon baking powder
3 tablespoons smooth (no pulp)
  orange juice

Preheat the oven to 350°F.

First, make the filling. Break the chocolate into squares and place them in the top of a double-boiler or in a small, heatproof bowl set over a pan of hot water to melt.

Once melted, remove the chocolate from the heat and add the rest of the filling ingredients. Blend until very smooth.

To make the pastry, beat the butter and sugar together until pale.

While still beating, slowly add the egg yolks to the mixture one at a time.

Still beating, add spoonfuls of the dry ingredients until all used up.

Continue to beat until this is all incorporated, then slowly add the orange juice.

On a very well-floured board, pat out the pastry with your hands to approximately ¼-inch thickness.

With a 3-inch cookie cutter, cut the pastry into rounds and place them on a baking sheet lined with parchment paper.

Moisten the edges of each round (do one at a time) with water, then place a teaspoonful of the chocolate mixture in the center of each. Fold in the edges to form a triangular shape.

Bake until the pastry is a pale golden brown, 15–20 minutes.

Let cool on the baking sheet set on a wire rack before serving.

A wickedly delicious treat.

fritlach

makes approximately 30

1 ¾ cups all-purpose flour
1 egg
¼ teaspoon salt
1 tablespoon vegetable oil

about 4 tablespoons water
1 tablespoon clear honey
vegetable oil for frying
sugar for sprinkling

Put all the ingredients, except the vegetable oil for frying and the sugar, into a mixer or food processor. Beat or blend until you have a soft dough.

Dust a chopping board with flour and knead the dough on it for about 1 minute.

Cover with plastic wrap and refrigerate for 30 minutes.

Unwrap the dough and roll it out on a well-floured board until it is paper-thin.

Use a cookie cutter to cut it into rounds. Or, if you wish, cut it into crescents, or use your artistic flair to create other shapes.

Fry the shapes in the hot vegetable oil until pale golden brown on each side (this takes only a few seconds).

Place on paper towels to absorb any excess oil, then sprinkle with sugar.

A golden moment, best served hot.

posh pears

serves 6–8

8 large pears (e.g. Bartlett),
  peeled, but with stems left on
juice of ½ lemon
3 cups red wine

¾ cup sugar
2 cinnamon sticks
1 vanilla bean, split lengthwise

Put the pears in a deep saucepan and drizzle the lemon juice over them.

Mix the red wine with the sugar and pour over the pears.

Place the cinnamon sticks and vanilla bean in the liquid.

Bring to a boil and simmer until the pears are soft, about 40 minutes. Keep turning the pears during this procedure, to make sure they cook evenly.

When the pears are ready, remove them from the saucepan and let them cool in a serving dish.

Boil the liquid in the pan on high heat until it has reduced by half and looks like a thick syrup.

Strain and pour over the pears.

A dessert beyond com-pear!

the princess-perfect passover

Before every Passover, a Jewish Princess always asks herself three very important questions:

> Who is going to make Seder?
> Answer: Me.
> Who is going to clean out all the cupboards?
> Answer: Me.
> Who is going to fight her way around the supermarket?
> Answer: Me.

This is quickly followed by a fourth very important question:

> Can we go away this year?

Each year, before you know it, Passover descends upon us. You can feel it in the air: a change of mood, worry, and anxiety. Questions are asked—and these are not the ones in the *Hagaddah*, the book that tells the story of Passover. Who is going to make the Seder? This is a two-day annual event: a feast where we sit around the table, which is dressed in a white tablecloth and holding the Seder plate*, drink cups of kiddush wine, and continue the tradition of retelling the story of the exodus from Egypt.

Yes, we were slaves unto Egypt and we had had enough of bondage (I won't make a joke here). We escaped from persecution with the help of Moses and the Main Man, together with many miracles. Because of this, our JP ancestors made a speedy exit, leaving Egypt behind, to

---

*The plate of symbolic foods used at Passover.

wander in the desert for forty years. It was so speedy, in fact, that they had no time to let their bread rise (they didn't have electric breadmakers in those days); they simply carried the dough on their backs and it baked in the sun. So during Passover we eat unleavened bread, called matzo: a large, dry, FAT-FREE cracker.

Every Jewish Princess has to decide just how Princess Passover she is prepared to be. I mean, there is so much to do, from spring cleaning (personally, I love a bit of Passover feng shui) to "Changing Over." Changing Over means just that: changing over all your dishes, flatware, pots and pans, utensils, etc., to a whole new set that can be used only for Passover (a good excuse to hit the homewares department). Some Princesses line every surface of their kitchens, and others even have a kitchen that they open up just to use during Passover. Cupboards are emptied, and traditionally foods that you are not able to use during the holiday (these foods are called *chametz*) are sold for a token amount and then usually passed on to charity. So all new food is bought that has been cooked under supervision. You can recognize these foods because they all have a special label (I love a label) that shows they are *Pesachdic*—designed for Passover, that is, not Prada.

I have to confess that it is not only the preparation for Passover but actually the *keeping* of it that makes me ask, should I pass over Passover? I just can't help it, even when I know I'm not afraid of a little hard work —though I know you don't believe me. I love it when the house has been spring-cleaned (OK, so I have had a little *help*...). And I don't mind clearing out kitchen cupboards: It can be quite therapeutic, actually, and I always find something that is out of date. If I'm really honest with myself, sitting down for Seder night is one of the most special evenings of the year, and it gives me a strong sense of who I am and where I come from.

Yes, even the food during Passover can be fantastic, but my advice? Go easy on the eggs. I mean, you haven't lived until you have tried a hard-cooked egg in salt water (I know; it sounds disgusting), and as for coconut macaroons and cinnamon balls, these delicious sweetmeats should be eaten all year round.

But of course they're not.

I mean, it would be like eating pumpkin pie in August.

So now I have one more question to ask. Why do I panic at Passover? I suppose it's the *thought* of Passover that scares me (anyone else feel the same?). Yet, looking on the bright side, it's only eight days—not forty years! Your house is immaculate. Your Seder night will provide you and your children with wonderful memories, and with the help of my wonderful recipes for breakfast, savory dishes, and, of course, some Princess Passover sweet treats, just think of this festival as getting in touch with all those wonderful traditions that have been passed down from generation to generation.

This year I am going to make it a Princess-Positive Passover, and you never know: Maybe next year we'll be in Jerusalem.

Personally, though, I would like to be at the Royal Beach—in Eilat!

princess passover pointers

1. Princess Prepare. Making lists is invaluable. Mine are always very long!

2. When spring arrives, start using up everything in your pantry, your second pantry, and ALL your freezers.

3. Need to use up alcohol? Have a pre-Passover party, or donate booze to your local university or even your gardener (once he has finished work).

4. Received any wedding presents or gifts that aren't quite Princess Perfect? Keep them for Passover. When it comes to style, just think "eclectic."

5. Glass bowls, etc., can be used for cold milk or meat meals, so if buying new, GO FOR GLASS.

6. To line your kitchen cupboards, buy laminated material. Use tracing paper to make templates of your shelves, then use those to cut out the material.

7. Join a warehouse club. Disposable plates, etc., make life a lot easier, especially if you're greeted with one, two, or ten extra guests (like when the kids invite "just a few" of their friends). It may not be environmentally friendly, but it will make *you* friendlier—and you can always recycle.

8. Try to Princess Plan your meals for all eight days of Passover so that you'll order all the correct ingredients.

9. If you are invited to a Princess Pal's for dinner, take a lovely present and GO!

10. Even though the story of Passover is all about slavery, use the above Princess Pointers and make sure you are *not* a slave to your kitchen.

bobbie bagels

makes approximately 24

¾ cup non-dairy margarine
2 cups water
½ teaspoon salt

2 cups fine matzo meal
4 eggs
2 teaspoons sugar

Preheat the oven to 400°F.

Melt the margarine in a saucepan over low heat. Stir in all the other ingredients until the mixture resembles a chouxlike dough.

Moisten your hands with water. Take a heaped tablespoon of the dough at a time and form it into a ball.

Place the bagels on a baking sheet lined with parchment paper.

Make a hole in the center of each.

Bake until lightly browned on top, 30–35 minutes.

Perfect for lunchboxes.

bubbelehs (passover pancakes)

makes approximately 15

4 eggs
1 tablespoon milk
¼ cup fine matzo meal

vegetable oil for frying
¼ cup sugar
1 teaspoon ground cinnamon

In a medium bowl, mix the eggs, milk, and matzo meal together until the batter is smooth.

Heat the oil in a large frying pan.

Drop a tablespoon of the batter at a time into the hot oil. Repeat until the pan is full.

Fry the pancakes until golden brown, about 2 minutes, turning them over halfway through the cooking time to make sure the color is even.

When golden brown all over, lift out onto paper towels to remove any excess oil.

In a separate bowl, mix together the sugar and cinnamon.

When the *bubbelehs* are ready to eat, serve with the cinnamon sugar on the side, ready for dipping.

For a more sophisticated alternative, use a tablespoon of sweet red wine instead of milk.

matzo brie

serves 2

4 large matzos
3 extra-large eggs
½ cup whole milk
unsalted butter
2 tablespoons sugar

Break up the matzos into small pieces and place them in a large bowl.

Beat the eggs. Add the milk and stir the mixture, then pour it over the broken matzos. Let soak for 5 minutes.

Coat a large frying pan with melted butter and pour in the saturated matzo mixture.

Cook over low heat for a few minutes, turning over halfway through cooking. It will look similar to an omelet.

Divide the mixture in two and place each half on a plate.

Sprinkle each matzo *brie* with sugar before serving.

JP Junior's grandpa prefers it with salt, and JP Junior's brother prefers it with ketchup. You choose!

princess passover granola

makes approximately 8 large portions

5 ounces matzo
6 tablespoons clear honey
¾ cup hazelnuts
scant 1 cup chopped walnuts
½ cup pitted prunes

1 cup raisins
1 heaped cup chopped
  dried apricots
½ heaped cup chopped
  dried dates

Preheat the broiler. Bash the matzo into very, very small pieces.

In a frying pan, mix together the matzo crumbs and honey.
Cook over low heat until the matzo is thoroughly coated
with the honey.

Mix the honeyed matzo with the hazelnuts and chopped walnuts.
Place under the broiler and toast for 2 minutes, stirring occasionally
so that the mixture doesn't burn.

Let cool, then add the dried fruit and stir well. Store in an airtight
container until ready to serve.

*I have never been able to find a delicious cereal to eat during
Passover, so I devised this wonderful granola, guaranteed to
make a Princess Perfect Passover. Cover with milk or add to
yogurt and fruit. This cereal is so good that you might consider
crunching on it all year round.*

A word about gefilte fish

If gefilte fish were a football team, it would be in the least successful league. However, it would definitely have a very loyal fan base, which would either have loved it since childhood or developed a taste for it somewhere along the way.

Admittedly, this very unusual boiled or fried ground fish is not to everyone's taste. Even the orange and gray-white outfit (a bit like my washing) with a splash of deep purple that gefilte fish would play in would not be to everyone's taste. But like all underdogfish, gefilte fish can sometimes be a true winner. I can hear its fans shouting from the stadium: "Go, 'Filte Fish, Go!"

Whether traditionally made from ground white fish and matzo meal, boiled and served with a fish liquor and a topping of sliced boiled carrot, or fried golden brown and served with a side of *chrayn* (a hot, purple-colored horseradish sauce), gefilte fish is a true delicacy.

I have developed a taste for gefilte fish and I am an ardent supporter of this strange, badly dressed fishy dish. However, it *has* to be fresh. I am afraid that buying boiled fish in a jar, as you often find it, is simply fake fish. I really think that, if handled in the right way, gefilte fish can take on the big boys and be a real winner.

If I were the coach of this football team, my one piece of advice, when dealing with gefilte fish, would be "Handle with care." If not treated with kid gloves—or, in gefilte fish's case, rubber—you could be left with a stink on your hands that simply will *not* go away.

gefilte fish

makes approximately 85 mini gefilte fish balls

8 cups vegetable stock
(made with 2 tablespoons
bouillon powder)
4 carrots, peeled
2 onions, peeled and left whole
3 tablespoons sugar
2 pounds ground fish (equal
amounts of whiting, haddock,
and porgy)

1 teaspoon salt
1 onion, finely grated
2 eggs
scant 1 cup fine matzo meal
a sprinkle of white pepper

Combine the stock, carrots, whole onions, and 1 tablespoon sugar in a large saucepan. Bring to a boil and simmer until the carrots begin to soften, about 15 minutes.

While this is cooking, put the rest of the gefilte fish ingredients, including the remaining sugar, in a food processor and mix well.

With damp hands (use a bowl of water for dipping), take teaspoons of the mixture and roll into small balls, then place these in the simmering stock. Cover and simmer until the gefilte fish balls are cooked through, about 10 minutes.

Remove the balls with a slotted spoon and let drain and cool in a colander.

Keep the stock simmering for 20 minutes longer to reduce.

Remove the carrots and slice them into thin disks.

Pour the reduced stock through a strainer and let cool.

Place the gefilte fish balls in a serving dish, pour the stock over them, and set a piece of carrot on top of each fish ball.

Serve warm or cold with *chrayn*.

If you wish to fry the fish balls, place in hot vegetable oil and fry until golden brown. Don't forget to put on your extractor fan!

This dish works equally well as an appetizer. Just remember not to confuse them with your matzo balls and put them in the chicken soup…

matzo meat parcels

serves 6

for the parcel
10 matzos
½ cup olive oil

for the filling
2 onions, minced
2 garlic cloves, chopped
3 tablespoons olive oil
1 pound potatoes, peeled
   and sliced very thin
2¼ pounds ground beef

1 eggplant, diced
salt and black pepper to taste
½ cup golden raisins
1½ cups beef stock, made with
   one beef bouillon cube
1 teaspoon ground cinnamon
3 tablespoons chopped fresh
   flat-leaf parsley
2 extra-large eggs
2 tablespoons fine matzo meal

Preheat the oven to 350°F.

First, make the parcel. Take the matzos and dip each one for a few seconds in cold water to soften it, then wrap them in a dish towel. Set aside for about 15 minutes.

Meanwhile, make the filling. Fry the onions and garlic in the olive oil until soft and translucent.

Add the potatoes and continue frying. When they are slightly brown, add the beef and the eggplant.

Season to taste with salt and black pepper. Cook for 10 minutes.

Add the raisins, 1 cup of the beef stock, the cinnamon, and chopped parsley. Stir well.

Continue cooking until the meat is done, about 20 minutes.

Remove from the heat and stir in the eggs and matzo meal. Check the seasoning and adjust it, if necessary.

Grease an 8-inch pan with a removable bottom. Brush each softened matzo with a thin coating of olive oil on each side, then use them to line the bottom and sides of pan. Don't worry if the matzos stick out of the top; they will be used for the top of the parcel. Save two matzos for the middle of the top.

Pour the filling into the parcel, then cover the parcel with the two reserved matzos and any matzo sticking out.

Bake for about 25 minutes, then remove and pour in the rest of the stock to moisten the top of the parcel. Return to the oven to bake for 5 minutes longer.

Remove and cut around the sides. Then—and this is the best part —release your parcel from its pan and serve.

A gift of a dish for a Passover Princess.

rosemary and lemon chicken

serves 4–6

1 chicken, cut into pieces
1 bunch of scallions,
  roughly chopped
1 large sprig of fresh rosemary
1 small bunch of fresh thyme

1 small bunch of fresh basil
grated zest and juice of 1 lemon
salt and black pepper

Preheat the oven to 350°F.

Place the chicken pieces in a roasting pan.

Add the rest of the ingredients, seasoning to taste with salt
and pepper.

Roast for about 1 hour, turning the chicken halfway through and
basting from time to time.

*A summery chicken dish that has a Mediterranean feel.
Personally, I always like to feel that I am in the Mediterranean!*

cinnamon baubles

makes approximately 45

2 egg whites
2 cups ground almonds
scant 1 cup superfine sugar

2 teaspoons ground cinnamon
2 teaspoons *kiddush* wine
1 cup confectioners' sugar

Preheat the oven to 325°F.

Beat the egg whites until stiff.

Add all the other ingredients, except the confectioners' sugar, and beat until the mixture resembles a paste.

Moisten your hands with water and roll the mixture into small balls —roughly the size of a very, very large diamond or a walnut.

Place the baubles on a baking sheet lined with parchment paper and bake until a light golden brown, about 12 minutes.

Remove from the oven and let cool, but not completely.

While still slightly warm, place the baubles in a plastic bag, add the confectioners' sugar, and shake—the cinnamon baubles will turn diamond-white!

When completely cold, store in an airtight container.

I have to say I haven't tasted better than these, but see what you think. A gem of a cinnamon bauble!

coconutties

makes approximately 12

5 egg yolks
¾ cup sugar
2 cups dried shredded coconut

1 cup mixed dried fruit with
   semisweet chocolate chips
4 ounces semisweet chocolate

Preheat the oven to 350°F.

Beat the egg yolks with the sugar until pale.

Add the rest of the ingredients, except the chocolate.

Moisten your hands with water. Take a tablespoon of the mixture and mold it into a pyramid shape with a flat base.

Place the pyramids on a baking sheet and bake them for 10–15 minutes. Let cool completely on a wire rack.

Melt the chocolate in a double-boiler, or in a heatproof bowl set over a saucepan filled with simmering water.

Dip the base of the cookies in the chocolate, then place on a wire rack to set. Drizzle any leftover chocolate over the coconutties.

When baking the cookies, put them on a low rack in the oven to prevent the tops from getting brown. Store (if there are any left) in an airtight container.

grandma's matzo pudding

serves 10

7 large matzos
1 cup sugar
4 eggs
½ cup non-dairy
   margarine, melted
⅔ cup ground almonds
⅔ cup *kiddush* wine
1 baking or tart apple, peeled
   and grated

1 cup golden raisins
scant 1 cup chopped walnuts
2 tablespoons hot-chocolate
   powder
1 tablespoon ground cinnamon

for the topping
2 tablespoons sugar
handful of walnut pieces

Preheat the oven to 300°F.

Break the matzos into bite-sized pieces and wet them in
a colander. When soggy, squeeze out any excess water.

Mix the matzo pieces with all other ingredients (except those
for the topping).

Grease a baking dish that is about 9 inches square and
2 inches deep. Pour in the matzo mixture.

Mix the topping ingredients together and sprinkle over the pudding.

Bake for about 45 minutes.

*I was so excited when I discovered my grandma's recipe. It is
absolutely delicious: a JP Passover version of bread pudding.
You could fuel marathon runners on this wonderful dessert.*

"must-have" macaroons

makes approximately 35

3 egg whites
2⅔ cups ground almonds
1¼ cups superfine sugar
1 teaspoon almond extract

1½ cups sliced almonds, bashed
(I advise using a rolling pin
to bash sliced almonds)

Preheat the oven to 350°F.

Beat the egg whites until stiff.

Fold in the ground almonds and sugar and add the almond extract. This will form a pastelike marzipan.

Spread the bashed almonds on a flat surface. Moisten your hands in some water, take a teaspoon of marzipan, and roll it into a ball.

Roll the marzipan ball in the almonds, then place it on a baking sheet covered with parchment paper. Leave space between the macaroons, because they spread during cooking.

Bake for 10 minutes.

Remove from the oven, and let cool. As the week progresses, the macaroons will harden, so my advice is eat A.S.A.P.!

These are delicious all year round—not just Passover—and can even be served as a petit four.

princess plava

serves 8

5 extra-large eggs, separated
1½ cups superfine sugar
  (divided roughly in half)
finely grated zest of 1 lemon
  and 1 tablespoon of its juice

¾ cup matzo meal
¾ cup fine matzo meal
  (cake meal)

Preheat the oven to 350°F.

Beat the egg whites until stiff, then slowly add half the sugar.

In a separate bowl, beat the egg yolks and add the remaining
sugar. Beat until the mixture turns pale, then add the lemon juice.

Very slowly add the egg-white mixture to the egg-yolk mixture.

Add both matzo meals, tablespoon by tablespoon, to the
cake batter.

Fold in the finely grated lemon zest.

Place in a lined 9-inch cake pan with a removable bottom and
bake for about 1 hour. Let cool before serving.

A light and fluffy cake. Princess Plava Perfect, of course!

shavuot
festival of weeks/pentecost

Shavuot commemorates the giving of the Torah to Moses on Mount Sinai. This was the first time the rules of *kashrus* were written, so you could say that when the Ten Commandments were given and the rules of *kashrus* received, the first Diet Bible was published, quite literally, in stone. It's amazing how many JPs have stuck to the rules ever since. Who says we have no willpower?

Our Princess ancestors must have been incredibly resourceful; after all, traveling through the desert is hard enough, never mind then being handed a whole new set of rules to govern your life. I can't imagine being stuck in the desert without a five-star hotel and a credit card (mind you, I can't imagine being *anywhere* without a credit card). While busy organizing their new kosher kitchens, separating milk and meat with different dishes, flatware, and cooking utensils, those early Jewish Princesses avoided any culinary confusion by eating only milk meals—which is why, during the festival of Shavuot, it is customary to eat dairy foods.

When the Torah was given by G-d* (like a bridegroom) to the bride (the Jewish people), it is said that Mount Sinai resembled the *chuppah* (the marriage canopy) and miraculously blossomed with flowers and foliage. So to make yourself feel like a true Shavuot Queen, it is customary to fill your home with flowers and plants. You could even use this tradition as a good excuse to put in an order with your favorite florist.

I simply adore dairy dishes, and when it comes to Shavuot, it is my commandment to forget the calories, raid the cheese counter, and bring out the blintzes (see page 56). Of course, the Princess *pièce de resistance* is to cut a large slice or two of cheesecake. So in this chapter, follow my culinary rules and enjoy my top-ten dairy dishes. If you fancy adding your own Princess touch, go ahead. After all, *my* recipes are *not* set in stone!

*A JP writes G-d like this because she was taught never to take G-d's name in vain, even in writing.

potatoes lyonnaise

serves 8

2 cups heavy cream
⅛ teaspoon grated nutmeg
2 teaspoons garlic purée
salt and black pepper to taste

butter for greasing
2 pounds potatoes, peeled
   and thinly sliced
3 onions, peeled and thinly sliced

Preheat the oven to 350°F.

In a large bowl, mix together the cream, nutmeg, garlic purée, and salt and pepper.

Grease a baking dish. I use a glass one (about 8 by 3 inches) so you can see the layered potato.

Put in a layer of potato slices, then a layer of onions, and then cover with some of the cream mixture. Repeat this until you have used up all the ingredients (I make three layers), finishing with the cream mixture.

Cover and bake in the preheated oven for 1–1½ hours.

A little bit of French decadence. That's why I love French designer dishes!

princess spinach

serves 6

3 shallots, minced
2 tablespoons olive oil
1 pound fresh spinach leaves,
   well washed
2 tablespoons butter

½ cup pine nuts, lightly toasted
   in a dry frying pan
salt and black pepper
¼ cup freshly grated Parmesan

In a large frying pan, fry the shallots in the olive oil until soft.

Add the spinach leaves and butter. Cook until the leaves wilt
(this takes very little time).

Add the pine nuts and seasoning to taste.

Finally, add the Parmesan, stir, and serve.

Perfect as a "post-pump-class" treat.

spinach and ricotta tart

serves 10

1 refrigerated pie crust, softened
1 teaspoon olive oil
1 small red onion, diced
1 pound fresh spinach leaves,
  well washed

1 pound ricotta cheese
salt and pepper to taste
1 teaspoon grated nutmeg
handful of pine nuts

Preheat the oven to 375°F.

Use the pie crust to line a tart pan that is 11–12 inches in diameter. Prick the pastry shell all over with a fork. Line it with parchment paper and fill it with pie weights. Bake for 10 minutes. Let cool, then remove the paper and weights.

Heat the oil in a frying pan and fry the diced onion until soft. Transfer to a mixing bowl.

Put the spinach in the frying pan and cook until wilted. Transfer to a colander and let all the water drain away, pressing lightly.

Put the spinach in the mixing bowl with the onion, then add the ricotta, salt, pepper, and nutmeg. Mix well.

Pour the mixture into the pastry shell. Sprinkle with the pine nuts and bake for 25–30 minutes. Serve hot or cold.

Tart-tastic!

strawberry, feta, and toasted pecan salad

serves 8

for the salad
½ cup pecan halves
1 tablespoon light brown sugar
8 strawberries, sliced
4 ounces feta cheese, crumbled
1 head of iceberg or romaine
   lettuce, shredded

for the dressing
2 tablespoons olive oil
1 tablespoon white-wine vinegar
2 tablespoons low-fat yogurt
1 teaspoon sugar
½ teaspoon Dijon mustard
salt and black pepper

In a dry frying pan, stir the pecans in the sugar over medium heat until the nuts are well coated. Let cool.

Toss all the salad ingredients, including the pecans, in a bowl.

Mix together all the dressing ingredients.

Dress the salad just before serving.

A super summer salad full of goodies.

vegetable risotto

serves 2 as a main dish, 4 as a side dish

4 cups vegetable stock
1 tablespoon olive oil
2 shallots, minced
2 garlic cloves, minced
1⅓ cups arborio risotto rice

1 red bell pepper, minced
6 cremini mushrooms, sliced
salt and black pepper to taste
1½ tablespoons unsalted butter

In a large saucepan, slowly heat the vegetable stock over low heat and keep it simmering. In another saucepan, heat the olive oil and fry the shallots and garlic until soft.

Add the rice to the shallots and garlic and cook, stirring, for about 2 minutes. Add a ladle of stock and keep stirring until the rice has absorbed the stock. Keep doing this until you have used half the stock.

Add the red pepper, mushrooms, salt, and pepper. Continue adding the stock, one ladleful at a time. Once the stock has all been used up, the risotto should be ready. It should look creamy, and the rice will be cooked but still retain a slight bite.

Check and adjust the seasoning, if necessary. Add the butter and serve.

I've always been fascinated by risotto: It is so creamy and delicious. By using the two saucepans you will get a Princess Perfect risotto—and it is so easy!

coconut rice pudding

serves 8

¾ cup short-grain rice
¼ cup packed light brown sugar
3 cups milk

1¼ cups coconut milk
(I use reduced-fat)

Preheat the oven to 300°F.

Grease a baking dish of 5- to 6-cup capacity.

Place all the ingredients in the dish and stir to mix. Bake for
1 hour and 20 minutes.

*I love this dessert. However, for some people, seeing this
pudding brought to the table transports them back to their school
cafeteria. I cannot guarantee that their first experience of rice
pudding there was a good one, so you'd better make two
desserts, just in case.*

cherry-cheese blintzes

makes approximately 24

for the blintzes
3½ cups all-purpose flour
4 extra-large eggs
5 cups whole milk
olive oil for frying

for the filling and syrup
1¼ cups mascarpone cheese
scant 1 cup cream cheese
½ cup sugar
1 egg yolk
pinch of salt
1½- to 2-pound jar morello
    cherries in syrup, drained and
    syrup reserved

First, make the batter for the blintzes (crêpes) by mixing together all the blintz ingredients, except the oil, in a blender. Refrigerate for at least half an hour, or, even better, overnight.

To make the filling, mix together the mascarpone, cream cheese, 2 tablespoons of the sugar, the egg yolk, and salt. Carefully fold in the cherries.

Whisk the batter before using to ensure a good consistency. Coat an 8-inch round, thin frying pan lightly with oil (pour in the oil and swirl it around the pan, then pour out any excess and wipe around the pan with paper towel).

Heat the oiled frying pan and pour in a thin layer of batter. The crêpe is ready when the batter starts to bubble or come away from the side. When that happens, just flip it over to brown the other side lightly. The first crêpe is normally a disaster—just eat it!

As each crêpe is made, turn it out onto a baking sheet and let cool. Keep oiling the pan after every two crêpes.

the blintz

Preheat the oven to 375°F.

Take one blintz and fill it with about 1 tablespoon of the filling mixture. Roll up the blintz and fold both ends underneath to create a parcel. Place in a baking dish. Continue this process until the dish is filled.

Bake the blintzes until lightly browned, about 15 minutes.

While the blintzes are baking, put the reserved cherry syrup (about 2 cups) and the remaining sugar in a small saucepan. Bring to a boil and let bubble until the syrup has reduced and thickened, about 15 minutes.

Serve your blintzes with the cherry sauce drizzled over the top.

For extra calories, a lovely dollop of sour cream on the side makes this cherry-cheese blintz THE BUSINESS!

chocolate duo-oh-oh-oh!

serves 8

for the coffee-chocolate mousse
4 ounces coffee-flavored dark
  chocolate
2 eggs, separated
½ cup heavy cream

for the milk-chocolate mousse
7 ounces good milk chocolate
3 eggs, separated
½ cup heavy cream
grated chocolate of choice
  (mine is white) for decoration

Note: You'll need eight individual coffee cups (bone china, of course!). This is best made the day before.

Slowly melt the coffee-flavored dark chocolate in the top of a double-boiler, or in a small heatproof bowl set over a saucepan of simmering water. When the chocolate has melted, remove from the heat. Stir in the egg yolks, followed by the cream.

Beat the egg whites until stiff, then fold into the chocolate mixture. Divide among the coffee cups, filling each one a quarter of the way up. Refrigerate to set.

Repeat the whole process with the milk-chocolate mousse ingredients. Pour this on top of the dark coffee-chocolate mousse, up to the top of each coffee cup.

Grate on your chocolate decoration. Refrigerate until set.

Perfect for dinner parties. Junior JPs love it made with milk chocolate.

chocolate-sour cream cake

serves 8

1⅔ cups packed chocolate
   graham cracker crumbs
4 tablespoons (½ stick)
   butter, melted
4 ounces semisweet chocolate

2 eggs
½ cup sugar
1¼ cups sour cream
4 ounces white chocolate chips

Preheat the oven to 325°F.

Mix the cracker crumbs with the melted butter. Spoon into a
greased 8-inch springform cake pan and press down with a fork
to form an even base. Refrigerate.

Melt the chocolate in a double-boiler, or in a small heatproof
bowl set over a saucepan of hot water. When the chocolate has
melted, remove from the heat.

Beat the eggs and sugar together until light and fluffy. This takes
a few minutes; start the mixer on slow, then speed up and don't
Princess Panic. Add the sour cream and melted chocolate.
Stir in the chocolate chips.

Take the cake pan out of the refrigerator and pour in the filling.
Bake until the filling is set, about 40 minutes. Remove from the
oven and let cool, then refrigerate.

When you eat this, you will smile like the cat that got the (sour) cream.

mars bar cheesecake

serves 8

for the base
2⅓ cups packed graham
   cracker crumbs
½ cup (1 stick) butter, melted

for the filling
1⅓ cups cream cheese
½ cup mascarpone cheese
4 egg yolks

scant ½ cup sugar
¾ cup prepared caramel sauce

for the topping
4 ounces milk chocolate
⅔ cup mascarpone cheese
1 Mars bar

Preheat the oven to 350°F.

To make the base, mix the cracker crumbs with the melted butter. Grease an 8-inch springform cake pan, then press the crumb mixture evenly over the bottom. Refrigerate.

Meanwhile, make the filling by beating together all the ingredients, except the caramel sauce.

Pour the caramel sauce over the crumb crust and spread evenly.

Beat the filling well again, then pour it on top of the crumb crust. Bake for about 35 minutes.

When the cake is nearly cooked, start making the topping. Melt the milk chocolate in a double-boiler, or in a heatproof bowl set over a saucepan of simmering water.

Once the chocolate has melted, add the mascarpone and stir until the mixture is smooth. Remove the pan from the heat.

Remove the cake from the oven. Let cool for about 10 minutes.

Spread the topping on the cake and place pieces of broken Mars bar on the top.

Let cool completely, then refrigerate.

A cheesecake that is out of this world! A real favorite with teenagers, so when you ask them to tidy their bedrooms, make this cake and they won't look at you as if you have arrived from Mars!

rosh hashanah
& yom kippur

from feast to fast, with fast feasts

In the Jewish Princess's calendar, Rosh Hashanah, translated as "The Head of the Year," is closely followed by Yom Kippur: The Day of Atonement. This is otherwise known as the beginning of "honey cake season," or The High Holidays. What many people may not realize is just how "high" these holidays really are: Every Jewish Princess has the delight of enjoying not one, but two new years, because Rosh Hashanah lasts for two days!

Now, I'm all for enjoyment, but this quirk of the JP calendar also brings with it a seasonal disorder that gets into the head of every JP on the planet. Up to this point, it has slipped under the scientific radar, but once you're aware of its existence, it's really quite easy to identify by its unmistakable signs.

I only have to look in my local supermarket and see food shortages: a run on golden syrup and the disappearance of apple-pie spice and cinnamon from the shelves. When chatting with my Princess Pals, the topic of conversation starts to revolve around the moral conundrum of which family members to invite for lunch, dinner, or tea. I also notice Princesses who no longer walk with a spring in their high heels, but rather scurry around with a look of angst on their otherwise unlined faces, clutching lists and shouting down their cell phones while shlepping huge amounts of shopping bags (even more than a JP normally has). Yes, from the beginning of "honey cake season" until the very end of Yom Kippur, CCD can affect even the calmest and most organized Jewish Princess.

"So what *is* CCD?" I hear you ask. "And is there A Specialist for it?"

Here are the answers. CCD is uncommonly known as Compulsive Catering Disorder. I am sorry to inform you there is no doctor who has even heard of CCD, let alone can diagnose or cure it. But I have identified this Princess Problem and am here to put your mind at ease. In my Princess Professional opinion, you will make a full recovery, right up until Passover (see page 28), when I am afraid the symptoms will return and you will once again find yourself standing outside supermarkets half an hour before they open.

To recognize the symptoms and deal with CCD, one must only look at "learned behavior" (inherited from our Queen Moms) to know that it is perfectly normal to panic when your refrigerator isn't full and your cupboards aren't brimming over, just in case one or ten people turn up for tea. So when it comes to the high holy days, isn't it reasonable to expect this genetic behavior to reach new heights? Therefore, don't be surprised when you have invited twenty over for lunch, thirty for tea, and ten for dinner, and then you go and repeat the whole pattern by doing it again the very next day!

There is a certain amount of Princess Perverse Pleasure in inviting so many guests to one's table—or should I say tables? (Make sure you ring the rental company early.) I have listened to many conversations like the one below, over produce mountains as JPs unload their carts:

"How many have you got?"

"Sixteen."

"Lucky you. I've got twenty."

Then they roll their eyes and start unpacking their extortionately expensive cherries.

Well. It is a *yom tov*, after all.

spanish chicken

serves 6–8

1 chicken, cut into 8 pieces
4 medium tomatoes, cut
  into quarters
5 bay leaves
4 ounces kosher turkey kabano
  sausages, cut into
  approximately 2-inch pieces

1 teaspoon ground turmeric
½ teaspoon ground ginger
3 small onions, chopped
1 cup chicken stock

Preheat the oven to 350°F.

Put the chicken, tomatoes, bay leaves, and kabanos in a
baking dish.

Mix the other ingredients into the stock and pour this over
the chicken.

Roast for about 1½ hours.

Have a fiesta and then finish with a shluff (a Yiddish siesta).

roast beef

serves 10–12

6½-pound boneless beef
  rib-eye roast
1 teaspoon English mustard
1 tablespoon garlic purée

4 shallots, chopped
black pepper to taste
1¼ cups prepared beef gravy
gravy powder

Preheat the oven to 350°F.

Place the beef in a large roasting pan. Spread the mustard and garlic all over the meat. Arrange the shallots in the pan around the beef. Season the meat with black pepper and pour the gravy over the meat.

Cover with foil and roast for 1 hour. Remove from the oven and uncover the beef. Spoon the pan juices over the beef and turn it over. Replace the foil and put the pan back in the oven to roast for 1 hour longer. If you prefer your meat well done, I would suggest adding another 30 minutes to the cooking time.

When the roast is done, remove it from the oven and let it relax for 20 minutes (a bit like me) before carving. Strain the juices from the pan and add some gravy powder to thicken (according to the directions on the jar). Pour the gravy over the sliced meat and serve with the Yorkshire puddings on the next page.

Delicious served the next day in sandwiches with mmmmmustard.

yorkshire puddings

makes 24

olive oil for greasing
1⅔ cups all-purpose flour

2 extra-large eggs
2 cups soy milk

Preheat the oven to 400°F.

Grease two muffin pans heavily with olive oil and place them in the oven to heat for 10 minutes while you prepare the batter.

Put the flour into a mixing bowl. Make a well in the flour, crack the eggs into it, and add the soy milk.

Slowly whisk the ingredients together until a batter is formed.

Remove the pans from the oven and pour the batter into the muffin cups until they are three-quarters full.

Turn the oven down to 350°F and place the filled pans back in the oven. Bake for 15 minutes.

Carefully remove the puddings from the pans (they will be hot!) and serve with the roast beef as soon as possible.

The batter can be made the day before and refrigerated. Try not to eat the puddings before they go on the table!

champagne salmon

serves 4

for the fish
2¼ pounds fresh salmon (this
   gives a generous slice for
   each person)
¼ teaspoon dried dillweed
2 onions, sliced
1¾ cups sparkling wine
   of your choice
salt and black pepper to taste

for the crème fraîche sauce
2 teaspoons all-purpose flour
¼ cup water
½ cup crème fraîche
2 squeezes of fresh lemon juice
¼ teaspoon dried dillweed

Preheat the oven to 350°F.

Wash the salmon well and place on a sheet of foil on a
baking sheet.

Add the rest of the fish ingredients, then make a loose parcel
with the foil to seal in the fish. (Mine resembles a clutch bag,
of course!)

Bake for 10–15 minutes.

Unwrap your parcel and remove the fish with a slotted spoon.
Strain the stock and reserve for the sauce.

To make the sauce, mix the flour and water together in a bowl
until smooth. Reserve.

In a saucepan over low to medium heat, slowly heat the crème fraîche. Add the 4 tablespoons of the strained stock, the lemon juice, dill, and seasoning.

As the sauce begins to simmer, add the flour paste, then turn down the heat and cook, stirring, for at least 1 minute.

Remove from heat, and serve the sauce with the fish.

This dish can be served hot or cold.

Fresh and fancy fish. Don't forget to serve with a glass of Princess Pink Champagne. Lechayim!

chicken marmalade

serves 6

1 chicken, cut into 8 pieces
1 onion, chopped
salt and black pepper to taste

for the marinade
2 tablespoons thick-cut marmalade
2 teaspoons soy sauce
2 teaspoons white-wine vinegar
1 teaspoon chicken bouillon
   powder
sprinkle of dried parsley
1¾ cups water

Preheat the oven to 350°F.

Wash the chicken thoroughly and place it in a baking dish, along with the chopped onion.

Mix together all marinade ingredients, with salt and pepper to taste, and pour over the chicken.

Roast for 45 minutes to 1 hour, basting occasionally with the marinade. The chicken is done when the juices run clear.

The chicken turns a gorgeous golden color—rather like me after a spray tan!

celery root and apple mash

serves 8–10

2 heads of celery root, about
2¼ pounds in total, peeled
and cut into chunks
3 apples, about 1 pound in total,
peeled and cut into chunks

⅔ cup dairy-free margarine
salt and black pepper to taste

Place the celery root in a saucepan, cover with water, and bring to a boil. Simmer until the celery root is soft.

In a microwave, cook the apple chunks on high for 5 minutes.

When the celery root is cooked, remove it from the heat and drain. Add the apple and any apple juice that may be in the microwave cooking bowl.

Add the dairy-free margarine and season to taste with salt and pepper.

Using an immersion blender, blend all the ingredients together until the mixture is smooth.

Check and adjust the seasoning, if necessary, then serve.

Designer mash.

green beans and mushrooms

serves 8

olive oil for frying
1 large onion, diced
1¾ pounds green beans,
  trimmed
14 ounces white cup
  mushrooms, quartered

28-ounce can crushed tomatoes
1 cup extra-light olive oil
¼ cup tomato ketchup
1 teaspoon garlic purée
salt and black pepper to taste

In a frying pan, heat some olive oil and fry the chopped onion until it is lightly browned.

In a large saucepan, combine the cooked onion, green beans, mushrooms, crushed tomatoes, oil, ketchup, and garlic purée. Bring to a boil and simmer for about 1 hour.

Season to taste and serve.

A mean bean dish.

israeli salad

serves 6

4 scallions
1½ English cucumbers
2 beef tomatoes
seeds from 1 pomegranate
handful of minced fresh
   flat-leaf parsley

grated zest and juice
   of 1 lemon
1 teaspoon salt
1 tablespoon virgin olive oil

Chop all the vegetables into tiny pieces and place in
a serving bowl.

Add the pomegranate, parsley, and lemon zest and juice.

Mix the salt and olive oil together and pour over the salad.

Toss well before serving.

The key to this salad is chop, chop, chop!

lime and apple slaw

serves 6

1 small head of white cabbage, approximately 2 pounds, shredded
1½–2 cups mixed sprouts
juice of 2 limes

3 tablespoons light mayonnaise
1 tablespoon prepared creamy salad dressing
2 red apples, sliced very thinly

Place the shredded cabbage in a bowl with the mixed sprouts.

Squeeze the lime juice into another bowl and mix with the mayonnaise and salad dressing.

Add the sliced apples to the cabbage, then mix in the mayonnaise dressing.

Keep refrigerated until ready to serve.

Very light and refreshing: great to munch and crunch on a hot summer's day.

princess-perfect potato kugel

serves 10

6 large baking potatoes,
  peeled and shredded
3 large sweet potatoes,
  peeled and shredded
1 large onion, shredded
3 extra-large eggs, beaten

5 tablespoons olive oil
⅔ cup fine matzo meal
⅓ cup sugar
1 teaspoon salt
black pepper to taste

Preheat the oven to 375°F.

Place the shredded baking potatoes in a strainer and weigh down with a heavy saucepan. Let drain for 10 minutes.

Put the shredded sweet potato and the drained baking potato in a large bowl. Add the rest of the ingredients and stir well.

Transfer to a greased baking dish that is about 14 by 8 inches.

Bake for 10 minutes, then turn down the oven temperature to 350°F. Bake for 1 hour longer.

This is a lovely alternative to serving roasted or baked potatoes and it tastes delicious. Also note that it doesn't contain any butter so can be used with meat dishes. Did you know that a South African JP is known as a kugal—"warm and lovely"?

princess potato salad

serves 10

2¼ pounds boiling potatoes
7 ounces smoked salmon,
   thinly sliced
1¼ cups sour cream

1–1½ cups diced drained
   dill pickles
1 teaspoon dried dillweed
salt and pepper to taste

In a large saucepan, boil the potatoes until *al dente*. Drain and let cool.

Slice the salmon into small pieces and mix it with the potatoes.

Add the sour cream.

Mix in the pickles. Sprinkle with the dill and season to taste.

Fold everything together thoroughly, then transfer to a serving dish. Chill before serving.

You might think that this is an odd combination, but it is truly scrumptious. I would serve this dish as part of a Princess buffet.

baked apples

serves 6

5 baking apples, quartered
  and cores removed
juice of 1 lemon
¾ cup golden raisins

3 tablespoons packed light
  brown sugar
1½ tablespoons unsalted butter
⅔ cup maple syrup

Preheat the oven to 350°F.

Place the apples in a baking dish and squeeze the lemon juice
over them.

Add the raisins.

Scatter the brown sugar over the apples and dot the butter
over the top.

Pour on the maple syrup.

Bake for about 30 minutes and serve hot.

A family favorite.

melon, pomegranate, and ginger salad

serves 8

2 tablespoons clear honey
¾ cup fresh pomegranate seeds
juice of 1 lemon
1 piece of stem ginger, drained
  and minced
1 tablespoon stem ginger syrup

2 canteloupes, cut into cubes
  (or use two different types
  of melon, if you like)
fresh mint leaves for decoration

Mix together all the ingredients, except the mint leaves, in a serving bowl and refrigerate until ready to serve.

Decorate with the mint leaves.

A fruit salad with all the special ingredients needed for a very sweet New Year.

ginger-beer cake:
a honey cake alternative

serves 8

1 ¼ cups all-purpose flour
1 heaped cup granulated sugar
1 teaspoon ground ginger
½ teaspoon ground cinnamon
½ cup nonalcoholic ginger beer

¼ cup vegetable oil
¾ cup golden syrup
2 eggs
2 teaspoons dark brown sugar
  for decoration

Preheat the oven to 300°F.

Beat together all the ingredients, except the brown sugar.

Pour the batter into a greased loaf pan (mine is approximately 9 by 5 by 3 inches).

Sprinkle the brown sugar on the top.

Bake for about 55 minutes, then let cool in the pan before unmolding and serving.

Similar to traditional honey cake, but I think even more delicious. In fact, it is so wonderful, it's dangerous!

honey cookies

makes approximately 35

¾ cup (1½ sticks) unsalted
    butter, softened
½ cup sugar
1 extra-large egg

¼ cup clear honey
1¾ cups self-rising flour

Preheat the oven to 350°F.

In a mixing bowl, cream the butter and sugar together until pale.

In a separate bowl, lightly whisk the egg.

Add the egg and honey to the butter and sugar mixture and beat until smooth.

Add the flour and beat well until you have a sticky dough.

Place teaspoonfuls of dough onto a baking sheet lined with parchment paper, leaving space for the cookies to spread (don't worry if they're not perfectly shaped; once they go in the oven, they seem to right themselves).

Bake until golden, about 10 minutes.

Remove and let cool before lifting the cookies from the paper.

Honey heaven!

jp honey cake: the secret's out!

serves 10

1¾ cups self-rising flour
½ heaped packed cup
  brown sugar
⅔ cup corn oil
¾ cup golden syrup
¼ cup molasses
2 extra-large eggs

juice of 1 lemon
1 teaspoon ground ginger
1 teaspoon apple-pie spice
1 teaspoon ground cinnamon
1 teaspoon baking soda
⅔ cup boiled water

Preheat the oven to 350°F.

Using a mixer, beat all the ingredients, except the boiled water, together in a large mixing bowl.

Add the boiled water when the mixture is smooth.

Pour the batter into a 10-inch loaf pan.

Bake for 40–50 minutes.

Unmold and cool before serving.

This recipe is steeped in security, and has been in the family for centuries, so you're very lucky that I've been allowed to tell other JPs about it!

banana, peach, and custard cake

serves 8

14 tablespoons (1¾ sticks)
   unsalted butter
½ heaped cup granulated sugar
2 extra-large eggs
1¾ cups self-rising flour

1 teaspoon vanilla extract
1 banana, sliced thinly
1 cup sliced canned peaches
1 cup prepared instant custard
confectioners' sugar

Preheat the oven to 350°F.

In a large mixing bowl, beat the butter, granulated sugar, eggs, flour, and vanilla together until the batter is smooth.

Grease a baking dish measuring 12 by 8 inches. Put half the batter on the bottom, spreading evenly.

Place a layer of banana over the batter, followed by the peaches. Pour the custard over the fruit.

Cover with the remaining batter (this can be quite tricky to do, so use a knife or spatula to help you spread the batter).

Bake for about 30 minutes.

Remove the cake from the oven and let cool. Before serving, sprinkle it with fairy dust (confectioners' sugar).

Try not to eat the custard before you use it for the cake!
Oooh, divine!

tarte tatin

serves 6

5 tablespoons non-dairy
  margarine
¾ cup sugar
juice of ½ lemon

2 pounds apples, peeled
  and quartered
1 sheet frozen puff pastry,
  thawed

Rub the margarine over the bottom of a heavy-based frying pan.
Sprinkle the sugar on top, patting it down.

Sprinkle the lemon juice over the apple quarters to coat. Arrange
the apples in the pan in the pattern you want in the tart.

Cook on low to medium heat until the apples are soft and
caramelized, about 50 minutes. Carefully turn the apples every
10–15 minutes during the cooking time.

Preheat the oven to 400°F.

Unroll the pastry on a floured board. Cut out a circle to fit your tart
pan (mine is 11 inches in diameter and 1⅝ inches deep).

Slide the cooked apples into the tart pan, then place the pastry
on top. Score the top and bake for about 20 minutes. Remove
from oven and let cool slightly.

While still warm, place a serving dish, upside-down, over the pan
and turn over. Your tarte tatin will drop elegantly onto the serving dish.

A classy tart!

succot

the jewish princess goes camping

Jewish Princes have very many admirable qualities. I'm just trying to think of some... OK, got it: They are *the greatest* dinner guests. When you cook for a Jewish Prince, he will be in raptures—especially if you follow my recipes. Be warned, though: He might compare your food with his mother's culinary skills, either in a good way or a bad way, depending on his mother's cooking.

Every Jewish Prince I know thinks he is a manager of a football team, or at least could be doing a better job than the manager of his favorite football team. Yet for all their *chutzpah*, Jewish Princes are generally brought up in THE JEWISH FAMILY, and therefore suffer with their own particular brand of Jewish Guilt. They can still make excellent husbands —*if* you know how to make them feel guilty *enough*.

However, if we are talking about someone to work the land, put up a shelf, or even assemble a piece of flat-pack furniture, DON'T ask a Jewish Prince. This kind of dexterity is not his forte. Which is why, when it comes to the festival of Succot, the Jewish Prince is severely put to the test. Not only does he have to don his outdoor gear (and this isn't a pair of swim trunks), he needs to be armed with a ladder and a toolbox. While the Jewish Prince probably has these, he might not know where they are. Once found, however, he faces the greatest challenge of all: building a new home called the *Succah* for his family and friends to enjoy.

Oy! And I thought putting up the shelf was a big ask!

Yes, the week-long festival of Succot, otherwise known as The Festival of Tabernacles, requires a *Succah*: a booth-like structure. Even though it is only temporary, it still has to conform to some very strict

building regulations. These include what height it should be, from what materials it can be built, and how the roof must allow visibility to the stars. The word *Succah* means "booth," and is a reminder of the temporary dwellings lived in by the Jews in their forty years of wandering in the desert following their escape from Egypt.

Obviously, in those days Jewish Princes had a little bit more expertise in the building trade. (I wonder if this is where we got the idea of pyramid selling?)

Anyway, throughout the week of Succot, it is a time to feast and give thanks for the earth's rich bounty and harvest. Invitations to family and friends to share and enjoy eating all meals in the *Succah* are issued, which means we all have to wrap up warm. (Unless, of course, it is raining—then the party moves inside.) To enable the family to sleep (yes, we do this, too) in the *Succah*, it is vital that the *Succah* is sturdy and SAFE.

Think about it: Even with all this partying, you don't want to bring the house down.

Dishes reflect the change in season and the mood of harvest festival. Both sweet and savory dishes are made from fruit and vegetables, plus stuffed foods such as stuffed peppers (see page 94) and *holishkas* (page 88), which is a dish of cabbage and ground beef, plus the "must-have" dessert for a Jewish Prince (especially mine): apple strudel (page 95).

So, when Succot rolls around very quickly after Yom Kippur, my advice is to make your Jewish Prince my wonderful apple and pine nut strudel and save a piece for the gardener, who I have a feeling might be in the garden with the Jewish Prince's ladder and toolbox, erecting a safe *Succah*, according to the building regulations.

A Jewish Prince asks a Jewish Princess
what her favorite fruit is.

"Well," she says, "I've always been
partial to pairs—of earrings,
shoes, handbags…"

challishing holishkas (stuffed meat parcels)

serves 8–10

2 heads of cabbage (fresh,
    then frozen: see method);
    Savoy is the easiest
2 onions, diced
2 tablespoons olive oil for frying
2¼ pounds ground lamb
1 heaped cup long-grain rice
salt and pepper to taste

for the sauce
2 tablespoons gravy powder
2 cups boiling water
3¼ cups tomato purée
½ cup packed brown sugar
juice of 2 lemons
grated zest of 1 lemon

Freeze the whole cabbages the night before, then take them out of the freezer just before you need them.

Preheat the oven to 325°F.

Fry the onions in the olive oil until lightly brown.

Put the cooked onions, ground lamb, uncooked rice, salt, and pepper in a large bowl and mix together.

Thaw the cabbages slightly, either by pouring hot water over them or in the microwave; this makes it easier to separate the leaves. You can also place the leaves in a large bowl and cover with boiling water so they are pliable and easy to roll.

Cut out the core of the cabbage with a sharp knife, then separate the leaves and wash them.

Take one leaf and place a tablespoon of the lamb mixture at the stem end. Roll up the leaf around the filling, fold the end over, and then fold up the sides to form a long parcel. Place, seam down, in a large, shallow baking dish.

Continue to make the rest of the cabbage parcels, packing them tightly next to each other in the dish.

To make the sauce, mix all the sauce ingredients together in a large bowl. Pour the sauce over the *holishkas*.

Bake for 2½ hours, turning the parcels over halfway through the cooking time.

This tricky dish, which is traditionally served during Succot, might seem difficult, but if you are challishing for a holishka it is well worth the effort.

lamb tagine

serves 6–8

2 cups chopped onions
3 tablespoons olive oil
3 tablespoons hot water
½ teaspoon ground cinnamon
½ teaspoon ground turmeric
1 teaspoon ground coriander
½ teaspoon garlic purée
4½-pound lamb shoulder
28-ounce can tomatoes

4 cups beef or lamb stock
1⅓ cups dried apricots
1 cup chopped Medjool dates
⅔ cup raisins
3 cups cubed sweet potatoes
3 cups chopped carrots
1 tablespoon clear honey
salt and white pepper to taste

Preheat the oven to 300°F.

Now before you Princess Panic at the long list of ingredients, stop, look, and listen. Most of these you will find in your pantry and it's just a matter of opening jars, cans, and packages. So here we go.

Fry the onions in olive oil until translucent in a large *shissel* or cooking pot—one that's big enough to hold your lamb and fit in your oven.

Mix in the hot water, cinnamon, turmeric, coriander, and garlic purée. Rub together to make a paste, then rub this into the lamb.

Brown the lamb in olive oil to sear it all over. Add all the rest of the ingredients and transfer to the preheated oven. Cook until the lamb is tender, 3–4 hours.

A very simple way of creating this exotic dish.

lemon-chile chops

serves 4

12 lamb chops
salt and black pepper to taste
grated zest and juice of 1 lemon
½ tablespoon garlic purée
4 stems fresh rosemary

1½ fresh, hot, green chile
peppers, minced (use more or
less chile, depending on how
hot you like it)
olive oil for frying

Wash the chops and season with salt and black pepper.

Mix together all the rest of the ingredients, except the olive oil,
and pour over the chops. Let marinate in the refrigerator for at
least 1 hour.

Preheat the broiler. Heat a small amount of olive oil in a frying
pan—use enough to coat the pan.

Put in the chops and fry until the meat is seared on both sides.

Place under the broiler and cook to the desired degree of
doneness, turning the chops over once during cooking.

*If it's hot, grill over coals outdoors. Serve with a crisp, crunchy
salad and a chilled glass of wine: lovely!*

sweet-and-sour meatballs

makes approximately 45 mini meatballs

for the meatballs
1 pound ground beef
grated zest of 1 lemon
1 extra-large egg
1 red onion, grated
1 tablespoon mirin
  (a sweet Japanese rice wine)
⅔ cup fine matzo meal
pinch of red-pepper flakes
  (optional)
1 tablespoon tomato paste
1 teaspoon ground coriander
1 teaspoon dried parsley
salt and black pepper to taste

for the sauce
28-ounce can crushed tomatoes
1 tablespoon tomato paste
2 tablespoons ketchup
1½ cups chopped canned
  pineapple in pineapple juice
1 tablespoon sugar
1 tablespoon red-wine vinegar
1 cup water
1 teaspoon dried parsley

Combine all the meatball ingredients in a bowl.

Moisten your hands with water, then take a teaspoon of the mixture and shape into a ball. Repeat until all the meatball mixture is used up.

Place all the meatballs in a saucepan of salted water and bring to a boil. Simmer for about 40 minutes. Remove the meatballs from the water with a slotted spoon.

To make the sauce, combine all the sauce ingredients, with
salt and pepper to taste, in a saucepan and simmer for about
40 minutes. Check and adjust the seasoning, if necessary.
If you want a more intense flavor, simply cook the sauce for
a little longer. If it becomes a bit too thick, add more water.

Add the meatballs to the sauce, turn to coat, and serve. You
can prepare this dish early, then simply reheat it.

This dish has so many flavors, it really Princess Perks you up!

princess stuffed vegetarian peppers

serves 8

8 bell peppers (choose a variety
  of colors), whole but deseeded;
  reserve the tops
2 onions, diced
2 tablespoons olive oil
1 small eggplant, peeled and
  chopped finely
4 cups sliced button mushrooms

1 teaspoon garlic purée
1 tablespoon paprika
4 ounces Brie cheese, chopped
  into small pieces
1 heaped cup long-grain rice
about 1 cup vegetable stock
salt and black pepper to taste

Preheat the oven to 375°F. Place the peppers in a baking dish,
standing them upright side by side.

In a large frying pan, fry the onions in the olive oil until translucent.
Add the eggplant and mushrooms, followed by the garlic purée
and paprika. Keep stirring the vegetables until they become soft.
Transfer to a dish. When cool, stir in the Brie.

Boil the rice with the vegetable stock, according to the package
directions. Drain and cool. Stir in the vegetables and season to taste.

Fill the peppers with the rice mixture and cover each with its
reserved top. Bake for about 40 minutes.

A wealth of health!

apple and pine nut strudel

serves 6

2 cups peeled and chopped
  apples (I use Gala)
⅓ cup apricot preserves
⅓ cup raisins
⅓ cup pine nuts

grated zest and juice
  of ½ small lemon
12 ounces pie crust (refrigerated
  or homemade)
confectioners' sugar to decorate

Preheat the oven to 400°F.

Put the apples into a mixing bowl. Add the rest of the ingredients,
except the pastry and confectioners' sugar, and mix well.

Roll out the pastry on a baking sheet covered with
parchment paper.

Spoon the strudel mixture along the center of the pastry sheet.

Join the ends together to form a strudel, then score the top.

Bake for 10 minutes, then turn down the oven temperature to
325°F and bake for 20 minutes longer.

Let cool, then sprinkle with fairy dust (confectioners' sugar).

A JP twist on the classic apple strudel.

pear and chocolate crisp

serves 6–8

8 pears, peeled and quartered
grated zest and juice
  of 1 lemon
¼ cup packed light brown sugar
¼ cup water
4 ounces semisweet chocolate,
  broken into pieces

for the topping
¾ cup (1½ sticks) butter or
  dairy-free margarine,
  chilled and diced
1⅓ cups all-purpose flour
1¼ cups rolled oats
1 cup plus 2 tablespoons
  packed light brown sugar
4 ounces semisweet chocolate,
  broken into pieces

Preheat the oven to 325°F.

Put the pears, lemon zest and juice, sugar, and water into a
saucepan over low heat.

Cook until the pears are tender, about 10 minutes. Gently stir the
pears from time to time to ensure they are covered by the liquid.

Transfer the pears and liquid to a baking dish and scatter the
broken chocolate pieces over them.

To make the topping, rub together the butter and flour, then stir in
the rest of the topping ingredients to make a crumbly mixture.

Sprinkle this crumbly mixture over the top of the pears.

Bake for about 25 minutes.

Serve with vanilla ice cream or whipped cream.

A truly lovely combination that everyone adores.

perfect peach kuchen

serves 8–10

6 large peaches, sliced
3 tablespoons Marsala
¾ cup dairy-free margarine
¾ cup packed dark brown sugar
1 cup plus 3 tablespoons
   self-rising flour
2 extra-large eggs

for the topping
8 prepared individual
   meringue shells
1 cup ground almonds
¾ cup sliced almonds

Preheat the oven to 350°F.

Put the sliced peaches into a bowl and drizzle the Marsala over
them. Set aside to soak.

Grease a large baking dish—mine is approximately
20 by 14 inches.

Using a mixer, beat together the margarine, sugar, flour, and
eggs. Spread the batter on the bottom of the baking dish.

Put the soaked peaches, together with any remaining Marsala,
on top of the batter.

Break the meringues into a bowl and blend them with the ground
almonds (use a mixer) until the meringue looks like small nuggets.
Be careful not to overdo it, though; you don't want crumbs!

Pour the meringue and almond mixture over the peaches.

Scatter the sliced almonds over the meringue topping.

Bake for 30–40 minutes.

Serve immediately.

This is best eaten as soon as it is made, because the liquid can make the meringue soggy if it is left to stand for too long.

strudel cookies

makes approximately 80

for the dough
3 cups all-purpose flour
1 cup (2 sticks) unsalted butter
¾ cup plus 2 tablespoons
   granulated sugar
2 extra-large eggs

for the filling
about 6 tablespoons seedless
   raspberry jam
1½ teaspoons ground cinnamon

3 cups mixed chopped dried fruit
6 teaspoons unsweetened
   cocoa powder

for the topping
1 egg, beaten
3 teaspoons granulated sugar
1½ teaspoons ground cinnamon
confectioners' sugar for decoration

Preheat the oven to 350°F.

Mix together the flour, butter, sugar, and eggs until a dough is
formed. Divide the dough into three pieces.

Take one piece and roll it out on a floured dish towel. (Do not
use a ridged dish towel or you will get grooves in the dough!)
Your pastry sheet should be approximately 16 inches long,
10 inches wide, and ¼ inch thick.

Spread a thin layer of jam (about 2 tablespoons) over the dough.

Dust ½ teaspoon of cinnamon over the jam.

Sprinkle 1 cup of mixed fruit over the jam and cinnamon.

Dust the fruit with 2 teaspoons of cocoa powder. Line a baking sheet with parchment paper.

Take the ends of the dish towel and roll up the pastry into a jelly-roll shape, then transfer the strudel onto the baking sheet. If you feel the strudel is too big to transfer, cut it in half.

Brush some beaten egg over the strudel.

Mix 1 teaspoon of granulated sugar with ½ teaspoon of cinnamon, and sprinkle over the egg wash.

Repeat this procedure to make two more strudels.

Using a sharp knife, cut the strudels at an angle into ¾-inch lengths, cutting only three-quarters of the way down and not all the way through the base.

Bake for about 20 minutes.

Remove from the oven and cut the strudels all the way through to separate the cookies. Dust liberally with confectioners' sugar.

Once you have the hang of these, they're not as daunting as you think. I was even surprised that fussy Junior Princesses adored them!

hanukkah

the festival of lights

Whatever age you may be—or, if you're a Jewish Princess, whatever age you may *admit* to being—Hanukkah (or Hanukah, Chanukah, or Chanukkah, depending on where you're from) holds the magic key that unlocks the child in all of us. This eight-day-long festival is filled with songs; my all-time favorite is *Moaz Tzur yeshu'ati:* "The Cat's in the Cupboard and You Can't Catch Me." There is the symbolic lighting of the *menorah*, the nine-branched candelabra that marks each of the eight nights—one head candle known as the *Shamas* lights all the others. Then there are the indulgent fried foods that are eaten and, of course (did I mention?), the Princess Presents that are exchanged.

It really is a festival of miracles. First, the story of Hanukkah centers on Judah Maccabee, who led his army to win a great victory over the Syrians. Why is this a miracle? Jewish men are not particularly known for their warriorlike skills—well, not in my house, anyway. After the battle was won, the Maccabees entered the temple in Jerusalem and completely cleaned it from to top to toe, removing all idols and rededicating it to G-d (the word *Hanukkah* means "rededication"). Once again, this is indeed a miracle: I can't even get my men to clean the bathroom sink!

To rededicate the temple, sacred oil was used to light the eternal flame. Unfortunately, they only had enough oil for one night, but miraculously it lasted for eight, so every year it is marked and celebrated with the Festival of Lights, otherwise known as Hanukkah.

Now, because I am The Jewish Princess, I want to talk about the Princess Presents and the fabulous food that is eaten over this holiday—and did I mention the Princess Presents?

It really is another miracle if you don't put on weight during this festival. After all, what can be more delicious than to feast on fried foods? From the potato pancakes known as *latkes* (page 110) dipped into apple sauce, sour cream, or even ketchup, to mouthwatering doughnuts of any flavor (try my Cheater's Doughnuts on page 112), not to mention carefully unwrapping the chocolate money that is traditionally given, nibbling around the sides and then letting the center melt in your mouth...

Well, I did tell you this festival unlocks the child in all of us.

With regard to presents, some families just give money, known as Hanukkah *gelt*. Fine by me. Others create a Hanukkah chest (but relax: this doesn't entail a trip to the plastic surgeon) and give a small gift every night. You know what they say: "All good things come in small packages" —especially if they are from your favorite store. Sometimes gifts are only given to children. However, as I said before and will say again:

Hanukkah UNLOCKS THE CHILD IN ALL OF US!

So as you read this chapter, think of it as a Princess Present from me to you. I bet it will take a miracle for you not to get in the kitchen and start frying TONIGHT!

How does The Jewish Princess
celebrate the Festival of Lights?

She phones the hairdresser and makes an
appointment for a full set!

corn fritters

makes approximately 20

1⅓ cups self-rising flour
1 teaspoon baking powder
2 extra-large eggs
⅔ cup whole milk
1 teaspoon dried parsley

salt and black pepper to taste
3 cups canned corn kernels
vegetable oil (for frying)

Beat together all the ingredients, except the corn and oil. Be sure to season the batter well. Stir in the corn.

Pour enough oil into a deep-sided frying pan to fill it by one-third and heat it.

Take a tablespoon of the batter and drop it into the hot oil. You can fry about six fritters at a time, depending on how big your frying pan is.

Fry the fritters until golden brown, then turn them over to fry the other side.

Drain on paper towels before serving.

A good way for Junior JP's to eat their vegetables. This also makes a great change from potatoes.

feta fatter potatoes

serves as many as you wish

allow 2 small potatoes per
  portion, cut into quarters
  (wedge style)
olive oil
1 teaspoon dried oregano
  per portion

salt to taste
3 tablespoons good
  mayonnaise per portion
¾ ounce feta cheese
  per portion

Preheat the oven to 400°F.

Put the potatoes in a roasting pan. Drizzle olive oil over them
and toss to coat.

Sprinkle with the oregano and season with salt.

Roast until golden, about 40 minutes.

Mix in the mayonnaise and the crumbled feta cheese, then serve.

Fabulous, and well worth getting fatter for!

mini maccabiah balls

makes approximately 45

2¼ pounds potatoes
2 leeks, white part only
2 tablespoons olive oil
salt and pepper to taste

corn oil for frying
2 extra-large eggs, beaten
all-purpose flour

Peel the potatoes and cook them in boiling water until soft.
Mash the potatoes and let cool.

Cut the leeks into small pieces.

Put the olive oil in a saucepan and fry the leeks until soft. Add
the leeks to the mashed potatoes and season.

Moisten your hands with water. Take a teaspoon of the mixture
and roll it into a ball. Repeat with the rest of the mixture.

Heat some corn oil in a frying pan.

Dip the balls in the beaten egg, then roll them in flour to coat.

Drop them, a few at a time, into the hot oil and fry until
golden brown.

Remove from the oil and place the balls on paper towels
to drain.

Delicious served hot—and they also make great canapés.

princess tahini-fried chicken

serves 4–6

1 medium chicken, skinned
  and cut into 8 pieces
2 heaped tablespoons tahini
⅔ cup all-purpose flour

2 teaspoons smoked paprika
1 teaspoon dried parsley
salt to taste
vegetable oil

Preheat the oven to 350°F.

Rub the tahini into the chicken so that it has a "massage" all over.

Put the flour, paprika, and parsley into a plastic bag. One at a time, add the pieces of chicken and shake well to coat.

Season with a little salt.

In a deep frying pan, heat enough vegetable oil to cover the chicken pieces. Fry the chicken until pale golden.

Remove and drain on paper towels to absorb any excess oil.

Transfer to a baking dish and bake for about 45 minutes. Remove and serve.

This is KKFC: the Kosher King of Fried Chicken.

sweet potato and apple latkes

makes approximately 40

4½ pounds sweet potatoes,
  peeled
3 apples, peeled
2 onions, peeled

4 extra-large eggs
2 cups all-purpose flour
salt and black pepper to taste
vegetable oil

In a food processor, grate the sweet potatoes, apples, and onions finely. Add the rest of the ingredients, except the oil, and blend until smooth.

In a deep frying pan, heat enough vegetable oil to cover the *latkes*.

Take a tablespoon of mixture and use your hands to form it into a flat patty. Repeat, using up the rest of the mixture.

Fry the *latkes* in the oil until golden brown on both sides.

Latkes *with a JP twist that would also be fabulous to serve during Rosh Hashanah (see page 62).*

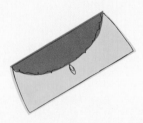

zucchini, italian-style

serves 8

4 zucchini
3 cups all-purpose flour
7 eggs

about 3 cups corn oil
salt to taste

Trim the zucchini. Cut them in half, then cut each half lengthwise into six slices.

Put the flour in a shallow dish.

Beat the eggs in another shallow dish.

Heat the corn oil in a large frying pan.

Take a slice of zucchini and coat it with flour, then dip in egg and then in the flour again. Repeat this method for the rest of the zucchini slices.

Fry the zucchini in the hot oil until golden brown on both sides.

Remove with a slotted spoon and place on paper towels to absorb any excess oil. Add salt to taste, then serve.

An Italian on the side that doesn't pinch your bottom. SHAME!

hanukkah cheaters' doughnuts

makes approximately 34

1 large *challah*, crusts removed
and broken into small pieces
2 extra-large eggs
2 cups unsweetened soy milk

1 teaspoon baking powder
vegetable oil for frying
sugar

Mix all the ingredients, except the oil and sugar, in a large bowl.

Once the liquid has been absorbed by the *challah*, blend the mixture with an immersion blender until smooth.

Heat the vegetable oil in a wok.

Drop tablespoons of the mixture into the oil and fry the doughnuts until golden on both sides.

Remove with a slotted spoon and place on paper towels to absorb any excess oil.

Roll the doughnuts in sugar while they are still warm.

A fantastic alternative to doughnuts that can be served any time, even for dessert—with fruit on the side just to make them seem a little healthier!

chocolate-cherry fudge

makes approximately 60 pieces

1¾ cups condensed milk
½ cup sugar
4 tablespoons (½ stick)
  unsalted butter

4 ounces semisweet chocolate
4 ounces milk chocolate
20 candied cherries, chopped

Put the condensed milk, sugar, and butter into a nonstick saucepan. Heat, stirring constantly, over medium heat until the butter melts.

Continue cooking and stirring until the condensed-milk mixture thickens and turns a pale golden color. You may need to raise and lower the heat now and again.

Melt the semisweet and milk chocolates in a double-boiler, or in a small heatproof bowl set over a saucepan of simmering water.

Mix the chocolate into the fudge mixture, then add the cherries.

Grease a pan that is approximately 9 by 12 inches and line with parchment paper.

Pour the fudge into the pan and smooth over with a damp spatula to get a nice even surface. Refrigerate to set.

When ready to serve, cut into small squares and EAT!

Fudgy, yummy, scrummy, and not good for the bummy!

chocolate truffles

makes approximately 40

7 ounces bittersweet chocolate
(70% cocoa solids or more,
depending on taste)
1 teaspoon Cointreau
(or liqueur of choice)

½ cup heavy cream
⅓ cup confectioners' sugar
1 teaspoon unsweetened cocoa
powder or ground cinnamon

Gently melt the chocolate in a double-boiler, or in a heatproof bowl set over a saucepan of simmering water. Remove from the heat and let cool slightly, then stir in the Cointreau and cream.

When cool, pour the mixture onto a piece of parchment paper and refrigerate for about 10 minutes.

Place another piece of parchment paper over a chopping board (I stick the parchment paper down so that it doesn't move).

Put the mixture in half-teaspoonfuls onto the parchment paper. Refrigerate for a couple of hours to set.

Place the confectioners' sugar and cocoa (or cinnamon) in a plastic bag. Add the truffles and shake until well coated.

Remove them from the bag. Place on your serving dish and keep refrigerated until you are ready to dive in.

Intense chocolate. Intense training the next day!

holiday fruit cake

serves 10

1 pound mixed dried fruit
¼ cup Scotch whisky
1 cup plus 2 tablespoons
  packed dark brown sugar
1 cup (2 sticks) unsalted butter

2 extra-large eggs
1½ cups self-rising flour
1 teaspoon apple-pie spice
½ cup whole milk
confectioners' sugar (optional)

Put the mixed fruit in a bowl and pour the whisky over the fruit.
Cover with plastic wrap and let soak for 24 hours.

Preheat the oven to 350°F.

Put the rest of the ingredients, except the confectioners' sugar, into
a mixer and beat until you have a smooth consistency.

Add the boozy fruit and mix well.

Grease a 9½-inch round cake pan. Pour in the cake batter.

Bake for 45 minutes, then remove and let cool.

Before serving, sprinkle with confectioners' sugar, if desired.

A Princess tribute to Uncle Eddie.

hot chocolate pudding

serves 8

for the pudding
4 large eggs, separated
1¼ cups 2% milk
⅓ cup unsweetened
   cocoa powder
¾ cup plus 2 tablespoons
   granulated sugar
1¼ cups self-rising flour

1 teaspoon baking powder
¾ cup (1½ sticks) unsalted
   butter, softened

for the icing
1 cup confectioners' sugar
2 tablespoons hot water

Beat the egg whites until stiff.

In a saucepan, heat the milk and cocoa powder together, stirring until you have a smooth paste. When the cocoa mixture has come to a boil, remove from the heat. Stir in the egg yolks one at a time, then add the granulated sugar.

Put the cocoa mixture, flour, baking powder, and butter in a bowl and use a mixer to beat until smooth. Fold in the egg whites.

Grease a microwaveproof mold that is 8½ inches diameter and 5½ inches deep. Pour in the pudding mixture. Microwave on high for 10–11 minutes.

Stir the confectioners' sugar and water together in a saucepan until smooth. Unmold the pudding and glaze with the icing.

You'll be taken back to a childhood chocolate-pudding moment!

caramel nuts

serves 6–8

pinch of salt
1 cup almonds
1 cup pecan halves

1 cup macadamia nuts
½ cup water
¼ cup sugar

Sprinkle the salt over the nuts.

Put the water and sugar into a frying pan and fry the nuts until all the water has been absorbed and the nuts are sticky.

Great served hot over ice cream.

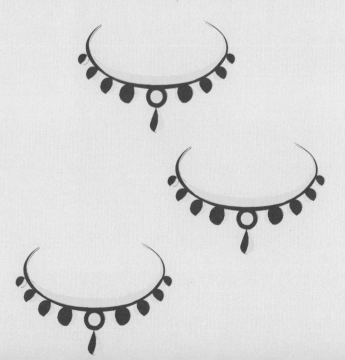

2

celebrations

the bris brunch

Once a Jewish Princess has gotten over the joy of giving birth to a boy—this could take a lifetime; I mean, you have to cope with the amazement that a Princess can actually produce a human who has different bits from her own—the inevitable Princess Problem of changing the diaper begins. Has this happened to anyone else? I hear it can be quite good for the skin... The next realization is that a Princess must prepare for the *bris*: the circumcision. Eight days after the birth, if all goes well and your baby boy is in perfect health, your house will be full of people watching a man tackle your son's tackle.

The *bris* (Yiddish) or *brit* (Hebrew) is every Jewish Princess's nightmare. Your son will cry, you will cry (I recommend waterproof mascara), your mother will cry, your father will cry—*everyone* will cry. Now I know it is supposed to be a time of great joy and celebration when your son makes his covenant with G-d (*brit* is the Hebrew word for "covenant") and is the most important commandment in the Torah, but truth be told, we are dealing with a protective Jewish mother, who will not let a fly hurt her new son, never mind an axe-wielding doctor.

OK, so I'm getting a little hysterical here with the axe part, but you know what I mean.

The *mitzvah* ("good deed") is that the *bris* should be carried out by the father—*if* he is qualified to do the job. (Mine has trouble putting up a shelf.) However, if not, this role is handed over to a *mohel*. For a Jewish Princess, only a top-class surgeon will do: a sort of royal *mohel*.

The *bris* ceremony is traditionally performed early in the morning and is a very formal occasion, the most important religious event in a Jewish boy's life. It really is a two-for-one, because as part of the ceremony, your heir is given his Hebrew name. A strict etiquette has to be followed, and members of your family are given different honors.

Your *bubbeleh*, dressed for the occasion in a designer nightie (for easy access), is placed on a special Princess Pillow. A Princess Pal who hasn't yet been blessed with children, known as *kvtarin* (g-dmother), hands the precious bundle to her hubby, the *kvater* (g-dfather). He continues the baby pass-the-package to your seated father-in-law, who has the greatest honor of all, acting as the *baal brit* "master of the circumcision ceremony," or *sandek* (Greek for g-dfather), who holds your offspring for the duration.

The actual circumcision is over very quickly; however, your mother and mother-in-law might have nail marks in their arms from where you have been clinging on. Then, as with any Jewish get-together, even in the case of a circumcision, food becomes a very important part of the day.

A brunch is served—but with NO SAUSAGES!

What did the Jewish Princess say to her baby?

"Gucci, Gucci, Gucci!"

bagel chips

makes approximately 16

4 bagels that are a couple
   of days old (any flavor)
7 tablespoons olive oil
salt to taste

½ teaspoon Cajun spice
½ teaspoon dried chives

Preheat the oven to 350°F.

Very carefully cut the bagels horizontally into four or five
very thin rings.

Mix the olive oil, salt, Cajun spice, and chives together
in a bowl.

Brush each side of the bagel rings with the flavored oil and
place them on a baking sheet. Bake for 40 minutes, turning
them over halfway through the cooking.

*This is a great way to use up old bagels to make a delicious
crunchy bite that can be used at any meal. I love serving them
at lunch with a variety of dips and crudités, but they can even be
served with drinks before dinner. Why not experiment with grated
cheese, flavored oils, and other herbs—whatever takes your
fancy? Store in an airtight container.*

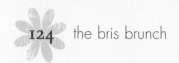

a collection of cream cheeses

each serves approximately 20

sun-dried tomato and basil cream cheese

1¾ cups light cream cheese
5 sun-dried tomatoes in
  extra-virgin olive oil, chopped

6 fresh basil leaves, chopped
salt and black pepper to taste

Use an immersion blender to mix together all the ingredients, seasoning with salt and pepper.

Keep refrigerated until ready to serve.

Dip or spread—have it on a bagel for a breakfast in bed (now wouldn't that be Princess Perfect?).

tuna and celery cream cheese

1 heaped cup canned tuna,
  drained
½ cup cream cheese
2 celery ribs, minced

1 shallot, minced
⅔ cup diced English cucumber
salt and pepper to taste

Mix all of the ingredients together in a large mixing bowl. Keep refrigerated until ready to serve.

Delicious on toast or in a baked potato—mmmm.

avocado and scallion cream cheese

4 scallions, minced (use the
white part only)
1 large, ripe avocado, flesh
scooped out

1¾ cups light cream cheese
½ teaspoon paprika
salt to taste

Use an immersion blender to mix all the ingredients together.
Keep refrigerated until ready to serve.

A green cream cheese that is good for the skin!

smoked-salmon cream cheese

7 ounces smoked salmon,
sliced into slivers
1⅓ cups cream cheese

juice of ½ lemon
1 tablespoon whole milk
black pepper to taste

Mix all of the ingredients together in a large mixing bowl.
Keep refrigerated until ready to serve.

The Princess Perfect accompaniment to the bagel.

tortilla princess-style

serves 6

¼ cup olive oil
12 ounces small cooked or
   canned potatoes, thinly sliced
   (2–3 cups)

1 large onion, sliced
8 extra-large eggs
salt and black pepper to taste

Heat the oil in a frying pan. Add the potatoes and onion to the pan and cook slowly. (This takes a while).

When the onions are translucent and the potatoes are lightly browned, remove from the frying pan and spread on paper towels to remove excess oil. Reserve any oil left in the frying pan for later.

In a bowl, beat the eggs with some salt and paper, then add the potatoes and onions. Let stand for 10 minutes.

Preheat the broiler.

Reheat the oil in the frying pan and pour in the egg mixture. Try to layer the potatoes in the frying pan; the smaller the frying pan, the thicker the tortilla. Let cook on low heat.

When the base of the tortilla has set, run a knife around the edge to prevent it from sticking to the sides of the pan.

Place the frying pan under the broiler, 4–5 inches from the heat source, for a couple of minutes to finish cooking.

Let the tortilla cool slightly, then unmold onto a serving dish.

The tortilla is best served at room temperature. When serving, slice into triangular sections, or, if serving with drinks, cut it into small squares and spear with toothpicks.

For something extra-special, why not drape a thin slice of smoked salmon over the tortilla and add a dollop of crème fraîche on the side? Don't forget the Champagne!

shakshuka: egg and tomato

serves 6

2 onions, diced
2 tablespoons olive oil
2 red bell peppers, cut into
  thin strips
3 cans (14 ounces each)
  crushed tomatoes
1 teaspoon ground cumin

½ tablespoon garlic purée
1 teaspoon paprika
1 tablespoon tomato paste
1 tablespoon sugar
salt and black pepper to taste
6 extra-large eggs

In a large, deep frying pan, fry the onions in the olive oil
until translucent. Add the bell peppers and continue frying until
they are soft.

Stir in the tomatoes, cumin, garlic purée, paprika, tomato paste,
sugar, salt, and pepper. Simmer for 30 minutes, stirring
occasionally. The sauce will thicken.

With the back of a ladle, make six small indentations in the
sauce and break an egg into each one.

Cover the frying pan with a lid and cook for about 4 minutes,
depending on how you like your eggs done.

Take the frying pan off the heat and bring to the table to serve.

Shakshuka *means "all mixed-up," and I know a few family
members this applies to first thing in the morning...*

muesli breakfast cookies

makes approximately 40

⅔ cup chopped dates
⅔ cup chopped dried figs
1 cup chopped walnuts
1 heaped cup rolled oats
⅔ cup self-rising flour
½ teaspoon ground ginger

½ teaspoon ground cinnamon
2 eggs
1 teaspoon baking powder
½ cup sugar
1½ tablespoons olive oil

Preheat the oven to 325°F.

Put all the ingredients into a bowl and beat with a mixer until the mixture comes together to make a dough.

Moisten your hands with water and roll the dough into small balls.

Place the balls on a baking sheet lined with parchment paper. Bake until golden brown, about 25 minutes.

Let cool on the baking sheet before serving.

Breakfast bites that will keep you going until midmorning—when you will be ready for a cup of coffee and another muesli cookie.

breakfast banana loaf

serves 6–8

1 cup whole-wheat flour
1 teaspoon baking powder
1 extra-large egg
2 medium, ripe bananas

1 cup mixed chopped dried
  fruit and nuts
½ cup clear honey
⅓ cup unsalted butter, softened

Preheat the oven 325°F.

Beat all the ingredients together in a large bowl.

Pour into a greased loaf pan (mine is 8½ by 5 inches) and bake for 30–35 minutes.

Unmold onto a wire rack and let cool.

A yummy way to start the day.

cinnamon cake

serves 10

1 cup (2 sticks) unsalted butter
1½ cups sugar
2 extra-large eggs
2⅔ cups self-rising flour
1¼ cups whole milk
1 ounce ground cinnamon
   (a small pot)

for the topping
1½ cups walnut pieces
¾ cup packed light brown sugar
4½ tablespoons unsalted
   butter, cubed

Preheat the oven to 350°F.

Beat together the butter, sugar, eggs, flour, milk, and cinnamon.

Spread the batter evenly in a 9½-inch round cake pan with a removable bottom.

To make the topping, combine the walnuts, sugar, and butter in a food processor. Blitz until the mixture resembles crumbs, but be careful not to overdo it.

Sprinkle the topping over the cake batter. Bake for 1–1¼ hours.

Be sinful: Have a slice of cinnamon cake with butter.

chocolate rugelach

makes approximately 20

for the pastry
⅔ cup unsalted butter, softened
⅔ cup cream cheese
⅔ cup sour cream
6 tablespoons granulated sugar
2 cups all-purpose flour
½ teaspoon ground cinnamon
½ teaspoon baking powder

for the filling
2 tablespoons unsweetened
  cocoa powder
2 tablespoons granulated sugar

to finish
beaten egg for egg wash
confectioners' sugar for decoration

Beat the butter and cream cheese together in a bowl until smooth. Add the sour cream and blend well.

Sift together the dry ingredients and add them to the butter mixture. Beat to make a soft, sticky dough.

Divide the dough into two balls and refrigerate for 2 hours.

Preheat the oven to 350°F.

Remove one ball from the refrigerator. On a very well-floured board, knead the dough for 1 minute.

After checking that the board is well floured, roll out the dough into a circle about 16 inches in diameter and ⅟₁₆ inch thick (you don't have to be too fussy about this).

Divide the circle into 10 pieces (like a pizza). Sift half of the cocoa powder over the dough and sprinkle with half of the sugar.

Take each section and roll it up, from the outside in, then curve into a crescent shape (like a croissant).

Repeat the same exercise for the second ball of dough.

Place the *rugelach* on a baking sheet lined with parchment paper. Brush them with beaten egg and bake for about 20 minutes.

When cool, sprinkle with fairy dust, a.k.a. confectioners' sugar.

The Jewish pain au chocolat.

The bar mitzvah

One day a Jewish Princess will wake up with her heart racing, in a sweat, knowing there is something she has to do—but what? Don't Princess Panic. This isn't a "senior moment"; you haven't reached old ladydom just yet. It is simply the realization that your son's or daughter's bar or bat mitzvah is just TWO years away! Which is why now is the time to open the bar mitzvah file and start preparing for this very special event.

Why do we Princesses Panic? Well, a bar/bat mitzvah is a very difficult function to organize. It is celebrated when a boy turns thirteen and when a girl turns twelve (well, we Princesses are always a little more advanced than our male counterparts, wouldn't you say?). At this special time, the child becomes a "son or daughter of the commandments" (this is actually what bar or bat mitzvah means) and takes the first steps into adulthood. This event is a very, very big deal in a Jewish family's calendar of events—and you need a very big deal to pay for it.

It is so easy to get caught up completely in the whole "bar mitzvah bubble." And if you're not careful, this event can take on a life of its own. Like your son (or daughter), it grows quickly from an idea to a representation of everything you have achieved and everything you wish and hope for in your son's (or daughter's) future.

So as your son opens his books to study his portion of the Jewish law, to *lein* (sing) or chant, depending on his voice (every Jewish mother hopes her son will have the voice of Pavarotti, the looks of Brad Pitt, and the intelligence of Einstein), or your daughter works on her *dvar Torah*, a speech relating to her week's Torah portion (every mother hopes her daughter will marry a boy who has the voice of Pavarotti, the looks of Brad Pitt, and the intelligence of Einstein), you can work out how many workouts it will take so that when you walk into the celebratory party,

wave to your guests, dance to that bar mitzvah classic "Reach for the Stars," in the mother of all mother-of-the-bar-mitzvah outfits, you will know there won't be even so much as a hint of the commonly known (and dreaded) "bar mitzvah bat wings."

Two years will fly by. You will become an expert in everything from chocolate fountains to life-size ice sculptures—all of which will stand you in good stead for future events, such as your daughter's wedding.

So in this chapter, please don't think I expect you to cater your son's or daughter's bar/bat mitzvah; you will have enough to do, what with hair, nails, and outfit-hunting. However, I have created 13 delicious recipes for you or your Princess Pals to make when you get together at the traditional pre-bar/bat mitzvah lunch to discuss that very important topic:

What *are* you going to wear?!

A Jewish Princess
is a Jewish Princess
all her life.

A Jewish Prince
is a Jewish Prince
until he marries a wife.

spinach dip

serves 8

3 cups chopped spinach leaves
2 cups shredded mozzarella
  cheese
1½ cups grated Cheddar cheese
1 cup crème fraîche

1 cup light cream
½ teaspoon grated nutmeg
1 tablespoon grated Parmesan
  cheese
tortilla chips for serving

Preheat the oven to 350°F.

Put the spinach in a saucepan over low heat and stir until the leaves have wilted.

Add the mozzarella, Cheddar, crème fraîche, light cream, and nutmeg. Stir until all the cheese has melted.

Pour the mixture into a baking dish.

Sprinkle with the Parmesan and bake for 10 minutes.

Serve the dip hot, with tortilla chips alongside.

Dip and quip.

hummus

serves 8

1⅓ cups drained canned
   chickpeas, rinsed
scant ½ cup olive oil
2 teaspoons garlic purée
6–7 tablespoons tahini
juice of 3 small lemons

2 tablespoons sheep-milk yogurt
salt and black pepper to taste
⅛ teaspoon ground ginger

Place all your ingredients in a food processor.

Blend until the mixture forms a smooth paste.

Check the seasoning and adjust, if necessary, then serve.

For dipping slices of hot pita bread.

easy eggplant pâté

serves 8

3 onions, diced
6 tablespoons olive oil
2 teaspoons garlic purée
2 eggplants (about 1¾ pounds
   in total), cut into small pieces
salt and black pepper to taste

juice of ½ lemon
3 tablespoons tahini
handful of chopped cilantro
3 tablespoons heavy cream

Fry the onions in 3 tablespoons of the olive oil. Stir in the garlic purée. When the onions are soft, add the eggplant pieces and the remainder of the oil.

Season with salt (you will need quite a bit) and black pepper.

Stir-fry until the eggplant is cooked. Remove from the heat.

Add the lemon juice, tahini, and cilantro and blend until smooth using an immersion blender. Let cool.

Stir in the cream. Check the seasoning and adjust it, if necessary.

Serve cold.

A rich pâté to dip into or spread.

pear waldorf salad

serves 8

14 celery ribs, "de-stringed"
   and chopped
3 pears, chopped
1 cup walnut halves
6 Medjool dates, chopped

1 orange, sectioned, plus the
   juice of ½ orange
3 tablespoons mayonnaise

Mix all the ingredients together in a bowl and serve.

A JP twist on the original.

edamame and noodle salad

serves 6–8

1 pound frozen shelled
  edamame beans
4 scallions, sliced
¼ cup toasted sesame oil
1 teaspoon soy sauce

14–16 ounces egg noodles,
  cooked
1½ cups minced cilantro
salt and black pepper to taste

Put the frozen edamame in boiling salted water and bring back to a boil, then drain.

Fry the scallions in the sesame oil and soy sauce for a couple of minutes until crisp-tender.

Combine the edamame beans, scallions with all the oil-soy mixture, cooked egg noodles, and cilantro. Season with salt and black pepper. Mix well, then serve.

This is delicious served warm. Edamame is what the Japanese call young soybeans.

coleslaw—hold the mayo

serves 6

for the salad
1 head of cabbage, shredded
1 heaped cup golden raisins
3 scallions, minced (use only
the white part)

for the dressing
3½ tablespoons olive oil
2 tablespoons white-wine vinegar
1 tablespoon lime juice
2 tablespoons clear honey

Combine all the salad ingredients in a large bowl.

Mix the dressing ingredients together thoroughly and pour
over the salad. Toss well.

Transfer to the bowl you are going to serve it in—and serve.

No mayo makes this Princess Perfect for a lowfat lunch.

sugarsnap peas, spinach, and chile salad

serves 6

for the salad
1 pound sugarsnap peas
4 ounces spinach leaves
8 baby tomatoes, diced

for the dressing
1 fresh, hot, red chile pepper,
  deseeded and minced
a large squeeze of
  fresh lemon juice
a slug of virgin olive oil
salt and black pepper to taste

Chop the sugarsnap peas, spinach leaves, and tomatoes, and combine in a bowl.

To make the dressing, put all the ingredients in a small bowl and mix well. Use to dress the salad and serve.

I haven't put specific amounts for the dressing, as it is up to each Princess to decide how spicy she would like her salad.

roasted butternut squash and red onion salad

serves 8

3 butternut squash, about
 4½ pounds in total
3 white onions, sliced thinly
2 red onions, sliced thinly
3 tablespoons olive oil

to finish
grated zest and juice of 1 lemon
1 tablespoon light brown sugar
grated Parmesan cheese

Preheat the oven to 400°F.

Wash the butternut squash, then bake them whole for about
25 minutes. Remove and let cool.

When cool, peel the squash, remove the seeds, and cut the
squash into about 1¼-inch cubes.

Put the onions and squash on a baking pan lined with parchment
paper. Drizzle the olive oil over the vegetables.

Turn down the oven temperature to 375°F and roast the squash
and onions for 25 minutes. Let cool.

Mix the lemon zest and juice and sugar together. Pour this
dressing over the vegetables and sprinkle with Parmesan.

*Partially cooking the squash saves all that bother of trying to cut
and peel this tough customer, so it's Perfect for Princesses.*

challah pizza

serves 4–6

1 *challah* that is a couple
   of days old (or use
   challah rolls)
prepared pasta sauce

for the topping
7 ounces feta cheese, cubed
   (or cheese of choice)
any other toppings you desire
handful of fresh basil leaves

Preheat the broiler.

Cut the *challah* lengthwise through the middle (do the same if you are using *challah* rolls).

Spread the cut sides with the sauce.

Add cubed feta and any other toppings of your choice.

Decorate with the basil leaves.

Put under the broiler, 4–5 inches from the heat, and cook until the cheese browns, about 5 minutes. Serve immediately.

Be imaginative. If you don't like feta, substitute another cheese, such as mozzarella. Be creative and use a variety of different toppings—anchovies, canned artichokes, corn…whatever takes your fancy for a Princess Perfect Pizza! If you want to make these into canapés, just buy mini challah *rolls.*

mozzarella and onion tart

serves 4

2 medium onions, sliced
2 tablespoons olive oil
1 pound refrigerated or
   homemade pie crust
2 tablespoons red-onion chutney
   (or chutney of choice)

salt and black pepper to taste
2 teaspoons dried basil
1 extra-large egg, beaten
4 ounces mini mozzarella balls
   (approximately 16)

Preheat the oven to 375°F.

Sauté the onions in the olive oil until soft and lightly browned.

Roll out the pastry on a floured board and use to line a 10½-inch tart pan.

Stir the red-onion chutney into the sautéed onions and season to taste with salt and pepper.

Spread the mixture in the pastry shell. Sprinkle with the basil.

Bake for 20 minutes.

Remove from oven, add the beaten egg, and dot the mozzarella balls over the top.

Bake for 10 minutes longer. Let cool slightly, then serve.

Looks fabuloso!

asparagus borekas (pastry puffs)

serves 6

13 ounces puff pastry, thawed
  if frozen
⅔ cup black-pepper cream cheese
  (if unavailable, mix black pepper
  into regular cream cheese)

12 medium-size asparagus spears
1 extra-large egg, beaten
handful of sesame seeds

Preheat the oven to 350°F.

Roll out the pastry on a floured pastry board into a rectangle.
Spread the cream cheese evenly over the pastry.

Put the trimmed asparagus spears in a saucepan and cover with
water. Bring to a boil and cook until crisp-tender, about 1 minute.
Remove with a slotted spoon and dry on paper towels.

Take two asparagus spears and place them, one on top of the
other, at the edge of one short side of the pastry. Roll into a cigar
shape. Trim the excess pastry with a sharp knife and use a fork to
indent the ends. Score the top of the *boreka* in three places.
Continue until all the asparagus spears and pastry are used up.

Mix the egg with the sesame seeds. Brush on top of the pastries.

Bake for 25 minutes. Turn the *borekas* over and bake 5 minutes
longer. Cut in half and stack at angles. Serve hot or cold.

*If you don't like the filling suggestion, try cooked mushrooms, onions,
pesto, cheese, or tomato—whatever your Princess pleasure.*

mushroom bake

serves 6

2 red onions, chopped
3 tablespoons olive oil
1¾ pounds mixed mushrooms
  of your choice, sliced
salt and black pepper to taste
2 teaspoons garlic purée
1 teaspoon dried oregano
2 handfuls of chopped fresh
  basil leaves

handful of fresh tarragon
1 cup mascarpone
½ cup ricotta
2 cups grated Emmental or
  Swiss cheese
14–16 ounces penne pasta,
  cooked al dente
6 ounces goat cheese, any
  rind removed

Preheat the oven to 350°F. Grease a large baking dish.

Fry the onions in the olive oil until they are soft. Add the
mushrooms, salt, pepper, garlic purée, and herbs. Cook until
the mushrooms are soft.

Stir in the mascarpone and ricotta. Remove from the heat and stir
in the Emmental. Add the cooked pasta and mix well.

Place in the baking dish and dot the goat cheese over the top.

Bake until you can see that the mixture is bubbling and the goat
cheese has softened, about 20 minutes.

*You won't have "mush room" for anything else after this
delicious dish!*

princess rarebit

serves 6

13 ounces puff pastry, thawed
  if frozen
4 extra-large eggs
3 tomatoes, sliced

1½ cups grated Cheddar cheese
  (or use your favorite cheese)
salt and black pepper to taste

Preheat the oven to 375°F.

Roll out the pastry on a floured board into a rectangular shape
about ⅜ inch thick. Place on a baking sheet lined with parchment
paper. Pinch the sides with your fingers (take off your rings!) to
form a rim all the way around.

Break the eggs, one by one, into each quarter of the pastry.

Place the tomato slices evenly on top and scatter the grated
cheese over the tomatoes.

Season with salt and black pepper.

Bake until the pastry is golden and the eggs are cooked, about
20 minutes.

Nosh on this while you get all the news.

The Jewish Princess
wanted to be the first to hold
a bar mitzvah in space.

Her only worry
was that it might
lack atmosphere.

the wedding

the princess and the prince

When I was a child, my favorite fairytale was *Cinderella*. I think it was the glass slippers I was attracted to. (Even in my formative years I was VERY interested in shoes.) I was so captivated by this tale that I would spend hours with my nose stuck in a Disney compilation, reading and re-reading, dreaming and pondering when, how, and where I would meet my Prince Charming and that most important question:

What would he look like?

So when did I meet Prince Charming? Well, like all fairytales, sit comfortably and I'll begin...

Once upon a time, I was dragged to a charity event to make up the numbers (not quite a ball, more of a cocktail party). I looked across a crowded room and saw a Prince who I thought was very handsome. I asked to be introduced, which was not my usual Princesslike behavior, but he had amazing eyes. My heart skipped a beat, but did he have eyes only for me? Did we dance until midnight? Was I wearing a pair of extraordinary shoes? No, no, and YES (well, I *am* a Jewish Princess.) He was there with another Princess.

DRAT! This story is not getting off to the best start.

So, are you wondering already, does my fairytale have a happy ending? Well, hold on a minute. This Princess had some work to do.

We became pals and dating began. He set me up with all HIS friends (this is getting worse) and every week I trudged out on blind dates, dressed for success (of course), but was tucked up in my bed before midnight—ALONE.

Well, just what sort of Princess do you think I *am*?

So time passed and Prince Charming was still seeing other Princesses (*OY VEY!*) and phoning to arrange dates for me with his friends. Did this Princess despair or give up? NEVER! But if this fairytale was going to have a happy ending, I knew that I would have to use all my powers of Princess Persuasion and steer him in the right direction.

I was used to getting my own way.

So I took drastic action and asked Prince Charming for his hand in marriage—ONLY JOKING! Actually, I asked him to accompany me to a ball (my Princess Pal was getting married). He accepted. He happened to be free that night.

He turned up *late* (some things never change). Can't we get anything in this fairytale right? YES, we danced the night away. YES, I was wearing a beautiful ball gown. YES, I had on fabulous shoes, and YES, he was finally beguiled by my charm! By midnight, Prince Charming and I were an "item," and he asked for my hand in marriage.

Well, not quite.

It did take two months, but then he proposed in his own unique way:

"I will be speaking to your father on Friday."

Did I accept?

I wasn't even sure if he had proposed.

So like all wonderful fairytales, let's cut to the wedding scene. It isn't necessary to get bogged down in the finer details, such as how do you keep two families happy, where are you going to live, and how are you going to afford to EAT? Let's move swiftly on and with one flick of my magic pink pen get to the fun part: THE DRESS, THE DRESS, AND THE SHOES!

Picture the scene: a warm summer's day (finally, something is going to plan). The stunningly beautiful Princess (it's getting better by the minute) has been bedecked in the bridal room; Jewish tradition dictates that Prince Charming has a look at his bride before the ceremony, just to check he is marrying the right Princess and not the older, uglier sister, as in the case of the biblical story of Jacob, Leah, and Rachel.

The Princess has walked (well, tottered) down the aisle to the sounds of a "Neil Diamondesque" *chasen* (singer) and an angelic choir, in her very high-heeled glass-ish slippers. There's an audible gasp from the congregation at her amazing, AMAZING dress (are you surprised?) and train (all six feet of it). She is followed by a procession of bridesmaids and page boys, all suitably (beautifully) dressed. She has released her arm from her father's vice-like grip and has circled her Prince seven times, to symbolize the protective care she will wrap him up in (she's never letting him out of her sight again) and that all barriers between her and Prince Charming are now waved aside (it's his lucky night).

After the seventh circle, she feels dizzy and exhausted (a sign of things to come), but this tradition has finally been completed—and let me tell you, it isn't easy with six feet of train.

She stands under a forest of flowers that adorn the *chuppah* (the wedding canopy), representing the home or PALACE (please G-d) that the Prince and Princess will build together. Her mother and future mother-in-law are looking fabulous in their dresses that DON'T clash (I told you I get my own way) on one side of the *chuppah* and her father and father-in-law are looking grand on the other.

The *erusin* (betrothal blessings) and the *ketubah* (the marriage contract) have been read and the Prince has promised that he will love, honor, and provide (he better) for his Princess according to Jewish law (the Princess stays *shtoom!*). The Prince and Princess have sipped the blessed wine. The rabbi has given his words of advice and told the Princess's father to "shut up" and stop sobbing—after all, he is not losing a Princess, but gaining a Prince (who can now pick up her shopping bills and boy, are they heavy!).

After a small hiccup (literally), the Princess waits for her new life to begin.

.

It is now the duty of the Prince to complete the ceremony by stamping on and breaking the wrapped glass. This is to remind the couple of the destruction of the Temple of Jerusalem, and that they must not neglect their moral obligations. She looks down, hoping he will succeed first time, otherwise their marriage might be cursed, and notices that he is wearing the most beautiful, BEAUTIFUL pair of Gucci evening shoes. At that moment, as the glass breaks, the photographer goes into a frenzy, the choir breaks into a rendition of "Sunrise, Sunset," and *Mazel tov*! rings out around the synagogue. The Princess knows that they are, like a pair of Jimmy Choos, the perfect fit and, like all wonderful fairytales, they will live happily ever after.

THE END

Well, not quite.

In the Jewish Princess fairytale wedding, food plays a very important part (of course). Before the bride has even been whisked off in her carriage from her parents' palace to the synagogue, the Princess bride's mother invites friends and family by royal appointment to *shlep naches*, wish her dolly *mazel tov*, and to see THE wedding dress. When the guests arrive, a table is groaning under a weight of goodies to welcome them. This is traditionally known as "The Table," and it is filled with miniature sandwiches and petite sweet treats.

So in this chapter I have used my Princess Powers and as your fairy godmother I have waved my magic Pink Wand to create food fit for a royal "Table."

May you all live happily ever after!

As she watched her
husband stamp on the
glass under the *chuppah,*
the Jewish Princess
knew that
this was the last time
he would ever put
his foot down.

how to create a jp sandwich selection

I have been busy designing my own range of Princess Sandwiches. Not only do they taste fabulous, but, of course, being designer, they look absolutely scrumptious. However, every Princess has different (but still elegant) tastes, so if you don't fancy the fillings I've suggested in this section, why not experiment? With so many delicious deli options, the list is endless.

Whatever fillings you choose, here are a few Princess sandwich pointers to help you create the perfect sandwich selection:

* Always remember to take your butter out of the refrigerator so that it is soft and ready to use.

* Invest in an electric bread knife.

* When the sandwiches are ready but the guests have not yet arrived, to keep your sandwiches Princess Perfect, lay some dampened paper towels, or a dampened dish towel, over the top of your sandwich selection to keep them moist.

* If you need extra sandwiches, just double the quantities I have given, depending on how many guests you have invited.

* When serving, use your designer touch and make these little bites as pretty as a Princess Picture. Give them space to shine: Remember, less is more. There will be requests for repeat orders, trust me.

the handbag sandwich

makes 10

10 slices of brown bread
unsalted butter, softened
10 ounces smoked salmon

1 lemon, halved
black pepper to taste

With a 3½-inch cookie cutter, cut a circle from each slice of bread. Spread each circle with a thin layer of butter.

Drape the smoked salmon on the bread. Using half of the lemon, sprinkle the salmon with a little lemon juice. Season with pepper.

Fold each circle over into a half-moon shape.

Take a pair of kitchen scissors and snip off any overhanging smoked salmon.

Thinly slice the other lemon half to make half-moon shapes.

Add a lemon slice to each sandwich, letting it poke out of the sandwich to create the "handle" of your "handbag."

A Princess creation that is so elegant to eat. Of course, in true Princess style, one handbag is never enough…

triple deckers

makes approximately 20

for the egg salad
4 extra-large hard-cooked
  eggs, shelled
2 tablespoons unsalted
  butter, melted
1 heaped tablespoon mayonnaise
pinch of paprika
salt to taste

for the triple deckers
20 slices of dark
  whole-wheat bread
10 slices of white bread
unsalted butter, softened,
  for spreading
10 cherry tomatoes, each
  cut into 3 thin slices
handful of watercress

Mash together all the egg salad ingredients in a mixing bowl.

Remove all crusts from the bread. Spread a thin layer of butter on all the bread slices.

To make each Triple Decker, use a slice of whole-wheat bread, butter-side up, as the base and spread with egg salad. Place a slice of white bread on top, butter-side up. Add tomatoes and watercress. Finish with another slice of whole-wheat bread, butter-side down.

Cut each sandwich into four elegant fingers (rather like mine).

Once, twice, three times a winner.

princess pinwheels

makes approximately 60

10 slices of white bread
unsalted butter, softened
½ heaped cup cream cheese

black pepper to taste
20 canned asparagus spears,
  well drained

Take a sharp bread knife (I use an electric knife) and remove all the crusts from the bread.

Spread each slice of bread with a thin layer of butter.

Spread a thin layer of cream cheese on each slice. Season to taste with black pepper.

Place two asparagus spears near the edge of each slice of bread. Roll up each slice tightly to form a cigar shape.

Wrap tightly in plastic wrap, packing close together to keep the cigar shape.

Refrigerate for a minimum of 2 hours (they can be kept overnight).

When ready to serve, unwrap the cigar shapes and cut each one across into six slices, forming little round sandwiches—and thus creating the Perfect Princess pinwheel.

Fancy, shmancy!

kosher wine kichels

makes approximately 60

2 cups all-purpose flour
1 cup (2 sticks) unsalted
　butter, softened
⅔ cup kiddush wine
　(or sweet red wine)
pinch of salt
1 extra-large egg

1 teaspoon vanilla extract
¾ cup granulated sugar

for decoration
½ candied cherry per cookie
2 tablespoons confectioners'
　sugar

Preheat the oven to 325°F.

Beat together all the ingredients, except the confectioners' sugar and candied cherries.

Using 2 teaspoons, spoon the dough onto baking sheets lined with parchment paper.

Decorate with the candied cherries.

Bake until golden brown, 10–12 minutes.

When they come out of the oven, dust with confectioners' sugar and let cool.

Store in an airtight container.

I know candied cherries are a little tacky, but to give this kichel an authentic feel, just think retro!

blueberry and sour cream sponge cake

serves 8

1 cup (2 sticks) unsalted butter
1¼ cups packed light
   brown sugar
2 extra-large eggs
1⅔ cups self-rising flour

1 teaspoon vanilla extract
3 tablespoons sour cream
4 egg whites
1 cup blueberries

Preheat the oven to 350°F.

Mix together all the ingredients, except the egg whites and blueberries, to form a batter.

Beat the egg whites until stiff, then fold them into the batter. Gently stir in the blueberries.

Pour the batter into a greased 8-inch round cake pan and bake for 40 minutes.

This is a great way of getting those nutritious blueberry vitamins into your system. They are youth in-juicing!!

florentines

makes approximately 21

7 cups cornflakes
2 cups mixed chopped dried fruit
   and nuts (even better if there are
   chocolate chips in the mix)
½ cup diced candied cherries

14-ounce can sweetened
   condensed milk
3 sheets edible rice paper
4 ounces semisweet chocolate

Preheat the oven to 350°F.

Put the cornflakes in a food processor and blitz until they have broken up (this should take only a few seconds).

Add the fruit-and-nut mixture, candied cherries, and condensed milk. Mix together.

Put the rice paper on a baking sheet. Take a heaped tablespoon of the mixture and place on the rice paper. Keep doing this with the rest of the mixture, leaving a small space in between the florentines.

Bake for 10 minutes.

Remove from the oven and let cool on a wire rack.

Break the florentines off the sheet of rice paper. (Each florentine will still have its base of rice paper, which is what holds the cookie together.)

Break the chocolate into pieces and put it in a double-boiler, or a heatproof bowl set a saucepan of simmering water. Melt gently.

Use a spatula to coat the base of the florentines with chocolate.

Let dry chocolate-side up.

Whenever you bake these, make sure you have guests coming, otherwise you will eat them all yourself as they are so amazing.

princess scones

makes approximately 14

3 cups self-rising flour
4 tablespoons (½ stick) unsalted
  butter
2 teaspoons baking powder

5 tablespoons sugar
½ teaspoon salt
6 tablespoons golden raisins
scant 1 cup whole milk

Preheat the oven to 350°F.

Mix all of the ingredients together, leaving the milk until last.
When you add the milk, do it slowly, because you may not need
to use it all to bind the mixture into a soft dough.

Flour a board and place the dough on it. Cover a rolling pin
lightly with flour and roll out the dough. The thicker the dough,
the bigger the scone will be.

Use a round cookie cutter to cut out the scones.

Place the scones on a baking sheet lined with a silicone baking
mat and bake until the tops are golden brown, about 10 minutes.

Serve hot or cold with butter, strawberry jam, and—if you want
to be naughty—whipped cream! Mmmmmmmm!

I promise these will all be "scone" very quickly.

triple chocolate chip cookies

makes approximately 36

½ cup plus 2 tablespoons each
   Demerara or Turbinado sugar
   and granulated sugar
2 extra-large eggs
⅔ cup softened butter, cubed
1 teaspoon vanilla extract
¼ teaspoon salt

3⅓ cups self-rising flour
7 ounces chocolate of choice
   (I use a combination of white,
   dark, and milk chocolate; you
   can even use chocolate candy)
1 tablespoon milk
confectioners' sugar to finish

Preheat the oven to 350°F.

Beat the Demerara and granulated sugars with the eggs. When
the mixture has turned pale, beat in the butter, piece by piece.

Add the vanilla, salt, and flour and mix well. Break the chocolate
into small pieces and add it to the mixture. Add the milk to make
a soft dough.

Lay parchment paper on a baking sheet. Using your hands, roll
the dough into small balls (approximately 2 teaspoons for each)
and place on the paper. Flatten each ball slightly with the back of
a spoon. The cookies will spread slightly, so allow enough room
between them.

Bake for 10–12 minutes. Sprinkle with confectioners' sugar while
still warm. Let cool before serving.

Mmmmmmmmmmmmmmmm with a glass of milk!

3

feasts

hosting the designer dinner party

When I give a dinner party, my aim is to be the "hostess with the mostest." To do this, my friends, family, and, most importantly, I (well, I *am* the hostess) need to *enjoy* it. After all, if I'm going to do all that shopping and cooking, I really want to get the "mostest" out of it. So when I throw a dinner party, of course I want to make it a Designer Dinner Party. I realized many years ago that Princesses just love coming over to my home to spend time away from theirs. They do not expect a "menu" when they sit down to eat; they do not expect a Michelin-starred chef in the kitchen. In fact, if you were that good, they would never reciprocate because they would be just too intimidated.

When you're in the kitchen creating, my advice is to find your own *signature style*—create a look that works for you. To do this, you may go through many different phases, but as all great designers know, there is nothing wrong with experimentation. After all, when you let your creative juices flow, you can come up with some culinary masterpieces. I admit that I've made mistakes along the way (just don't tell anyone), and that sometimes my food does not make the grade and has been cut (or thrown out) from my designer dish list. However, when Princess Perfected, my designer dishes look *haute*—but take note: They definitely are not.

When you think of fashion (a Jewish Princess does a lot of this), styles never really go away for good; they're just re-invented and come back in a slightly different guise. What you wouldn't consider wearing one season is top of your list the following year (skinny-leg jeans, for example). It's the same for a dinner party: One season a dessert is *passé* and the next it is the height of "kitsch-in" and back on the dish wish list.

To get you started, then, on the following pages you'll find some more of my top tips for hosting a successful Designer Dinner Party.

* Think about who you are going to invite. Your guests don't need to know each other, but the right mix of personalities makes a great cocktail.

* Make sure you are aware of any Food Fears or dietary requirements your guests might have. If you have a vegetarian, don't get edgy; I've included a delicious vegetarian feast on page 194.

* Write a list of what you are cooking and leave it somewhere you can see it so you won't forget anything.

* When deciding what to make, go for something you feel secure with. Remember, most people like plain, simple cooking and actually do not like rich, heavy sauces (hooray!).

* You can always buy in part of the meal. A lot of my Princess Pals leave out the first course and just serve more canapés, or even opt for a sensational sushi platter (purchased from a sensational sushi chef). I think this is a terrific idea, as it allows more time for everyone to relax (and maybe drink a little more of the pink stuff than they normally would —and yes, OK, I *am* talking about myself). However, if you enjoy good things in small packages (what JP doesn't?), then try making a selection of goodies from my canapé collection on page 174.

* Before your guests arrive, go through a mental check-list— something along the lines of the following:

> 1. Flowers arranged.
> 2. Candles ready to light.
> 3. Music on.
> 4. Pink stuff in the refrigerator.
> 5. Downstairs bathroom is clean, plenty of toilet paper, and clean hand towel.

6. Rooms sprayed with a delicious perfume.

7. Food is cooking; check the oven is actually on and at the correct temperature.

8. Leave time to look gorgeous: You don't want to greet your guests in your bathrobe. Or maybe you do. Who am I to judge?

9. Dress to impress, but make sure you don't *shvitz*.

10. If you wear killer heels, make sure that they are *comfy* killer heels (they do exist)!

* When it comes to desserts, it's simply unnecessary to recreate a dessert cart of choices. I just make one that is naughty (all the Princesses say, "NO," but eat it anyway) and always have another that is a fruity finale. Surprisingly, the fresh fruit is always most popular with the men. To make too many desserts spells stress—literally, it does: DESSERTS spelled backward is STRESSED—so beware. It is not *how many* desserts you make, but how delicious they are. I know I've done a good job if, after the first spoonful goes into a mouth, the eyes close, the chin tilts back, and there's a pause before "Mmmmm." This makes me a happy hostess.

Of course the end of a dinner party is just as important as the beginning, so I always serve a plate of Princess Perfect chocolates. Even though my Princess Pals cry out, "Oh, no: I'm full," it's amazing how their hands creep across the table to find that delectable treat. I gather my flavored teas, fill up the cafetière (marvelous wedding present), choose my mint leaves, and everyone sips and quips until it is time to leave.

So if you use the menu plans I have provided in this chapter, when the doorbell rings, smile, because you know what you have been designed to do:

HAVE A GOOD TIME!

a collection of canapés

green olive tapenade

4–5 slices of toast make approximately 20

1 ¼ cups pitted green olives
grated zest of ½ lemon
1 teaspoon chopped
  cilantro
½ teaspoon sugar

½ teaspoon olive oil
salt and pepper to taste
4–5 slices of bread (mixture
  of brown and white)

Use a blender or food processor to blend the olives until coarse-fine..

Add the rest of the ingredients, except the bread, and mix well, then refrigerate.

Toast the bread and cut into small squares.

Put a portion of the tapenade on top and serve.

A can't-go-wrong canapé.

blinis

makes approximately 42

2 cups buckwheat flour
1¼ cups unsweetened soy milk
1 egg
¼ teaspoon salt

2 grinds of black pepper
1 teaspoon baking powder
1 tablespoon vegetable oil

Beat together all the ingredients, except the vegetable oil, until you have a thick, creamy batter.

Heat the vegetable oil in a frying pan. When hot, pour away any excess oil.

Drop in about 2 teaspoons of batter for each blini. Cook until they dry and bubble, then turn them over and cook the other side. This takes very little time. Let cool.

When ready to serve, top with smoked salmon, a sliver of lemon, and chopped fresh chives or dillweed; or with sour cream, cream cheese, or any other topping—just use your imagination.

These look so impressive that your guests will think you have had the caterer in (stay shtoom!).

pizza straws

makes approximately 26

13 ounces puff pastry, thawed
  if frozen
¼ cup tomato purée
1 teaspoon garlic purée

salt and black pepper
  to taste
⅔ cup sliced black olives

Preheat the oven to 400°F.

Line a baking sheet with parchment paper.

Roll out the pastry and lay it on the baking sheet.

Mix together the tomato purée, garlic purée, salt, and pepper.

With a spatula, spread the tomato mixture over the pastry in a very thin layer.

Scatter the olives evenly over the top.

With a knife, mark down the middle, then mark each half into sticks roughly 1¼ inches wide.

Bake until golden, about 15 minutes. Use a pizza cutter to divide the straws. Serve warm.

A straw to adore!

a chicken dinner party

filled avocados

serves 8

2 hard-cooked eggs, grated
1 red bell pepper, finely diced
½ English cucumber, finely diced
salt and black pepper to taste

2 tablespoons olive oil
1 tablespoon red-wine vinegar
2 teaspoons garlic purée
8 small avocados

Put the eggs, bell pepper, and cucumber into a bowl. Season
to taste with salt and pepper.

Mix together the olive oil, red-wine vinegar, and garlic purée.
Pour this over the egg mixture and fold together.

Cut each avocado in half and discard the pit. Place the avocado
halves on individual serving dishes.

Spoon the filling into the hollows in the avocado halves. They're
supposed to be packed, so don't worry if the dressing spills out.

*Be careful when you remove the avocado pit using a sharp knife;
you don't want to end up in bandages!*

stuffed chicken thighs

serves 8

garlic-infused olive oil
4 shallots, chopped
20 button mushrooms, sliced
16 cherry tomatoes
a few slices of fresh, hot,
  red chile pepper

salt and black pepper to taste
4 handfuls of fresh spinach leaves
16 skinless, boneless
  chicken thighs

Preheat the oven to 350°F.

In a frying pan, heat a small splash of the garlic-infused olive oil.
Fry the shallots until softened. Add the mushrooms, tomatoes, and
chile. Season to taste with a little salt and black pepper.

When the tomatoes soften, add the spinach—the leaves will wilt
in seconds. Add a little more salt and black pepper, if desired.

Wash and season the chicken thighs. Place them in one layer
in a large baking dish. Spoon the vegetable mixture into the
center of each thigh and fold the thigh around this filling.

Rub a little garlic-infused oil all over each thigh, then turn them
skin-side up.

Bake for about 25 minutes.

*This smells delicious as it cooks. A healthy and mouthwatering
meal that is so quick, yet looks incredibly impressive.*

noo potatoes!

serves 8

24 small, new boiling potatoes
scant 1 cup sliced black olives
1 red bell pepper, sliced
1 green bell pepper, sliced
6 vine-ripened tomatoes, halved

olive oil
balsamic vinegar
2 garlic cloves, chopped
salt and black pepper to taste

Preheat the oven to 350°F.

Wash the potatoes and place them in a baking dish.

Add the olives, bell peppers, and tomatoes. Sprinkle with olive oil, a splash of balsamic vinegar, and the chopped garlic.

Season to taste.

Bake until the potatoes are tender, about 1¼ hours.

These potatoes are perfect for a dinner party: so colorful with a Mediterranean feel.

sesame sugarsnap and asparagus crunch

serves 8

8 ounces asparagus
10 ounces sugarsnap peas
2 tablespoons toasted sesame oil

1 tablespoon teriyaki sauce
1 tablespoon sesame seeds
salt and black pepper to taste

Wash the asparagus spears and the sugarsnap peas.

Remove the end of each asparagus spears and cut lengthwise in half.

In a wok, heat the sesame oil. Add the vegetables, the teriyaki sauce, sesame seeds, salt, and black pepper.

Stir-fry the vegetables for a couple of minute, then test the crunch. Serve immediately.

Crunch-eliscious!

cauliflower with a kick

serves 8

1 head of cauliflower, about
   1¼ pounds, cut into small florets
2 tablespoons olive oil
1 onion, finely diced
1 heaped cup cherry tomatoes

½ teaspoon ground turmeric
½ teaspoon garam masala
⅛ teaspoon sugar
salt and black pepper to taste

Cook the cauliflower in boiling salted water until it is *al dente*.

Drain and set aside.

Heat the olive oil in a frying pan and fry the diced onion until translucent.

Add the cauliflower and the rest of the ingredients. Fry until the cauliflower is tender. Keep turning to prevent the cauliflower from sticking to the bottom of the pan.

Check the seasoning and adjust it if necessary before serving.

A colorful way of serving cauliflower that looks great on the Princess plate! You can also make this earlier in the day and just reheat.

almond pudding

serves 8

6 extra-large eggs
1 cup sugar
1 teaspoon almond extract

1¾ cups ground almonds
⅓ cup sliced almonds

Preheat the oven to 325°F.

Separate the eggs. Beat the egg whites until stiff.

In a separate bowl, beat the egg yolks with the sugar and almond extract until pale.

Slowly beat in the ground almonds.

Fold in the egg whites.

Line a 9½-inch square pan that is 2½ inches deep with parchment paper. Pour in the batter. Scatter the sliced almonds over the top.

Bake for about 30 minutes. Let cool slightly before serving.

Can be served hot or cold. The taste is almond heaven.

clementines in caramel

serves 4

10 clementines or tangerines
2 cups sugar

1 cup orange juice
1 tablespoon brandy

Remove all peel from the clementines, keeping the fruit whole. Put in a heatproof glass dish ready for serving.

Put the sugar in a saucepan and add enough water just to cover —about 1¾ cups. Bring to a boil and boil until the syrup starts to caramelize, about 10 minutes. Turn down the heat and simmer until the syrup is light brown in color, about 20 minutes longer.

Take the saucepan off the heat and slowly stir in the juice. Bring back to a boil, stirring the caramel with a wooden spoon. Be careful, because it might froth up at this stage. Continue simmering for 10 minutes.

Just before you are going to take the saucepan off the heat, add the brandy.

Pour the caramel over the clementines. Let cool, then refrigerate.

After a couple of hours, turn the fruit over to ensure that you get a good coverage of caramel. Serve chilled.

This dessert is fat-free, so help yourself to two darling clementines!

a fish dinner party

mushroom soup

serves 8

6 shallots, chopped
3 tablespoons olive oil
2 pounds white cup mushrooms
2 tablespoons vegetable
    bouillon powder
5 cups water
1 teaspoon dried oregano

1 teaspoon dried sage
bunch of fresh flat-leaf parsley,
    chopped
4 teaspoons kiddush wine
salt and black pepper to taste
1¼ cups heavy cream

Fry the shallots in the olive oil until softened.

Add the mushrooms and fry until soft.

Add the rest of the ingredients, except the cream.

Bring to a boil and simmer for 20 minutes.

Blend until smooth.

Stir in the cream and check the seasoning. Reheat before serving, if necessary.

Garnish each bowl with a sprig of thyme.

halibut kabobs

serves as many as you like

4 ounces skinless halibut fillet
    per person, cubed

ingredients per kebab
¼ red onion
1 white cup mushroom

2 chunky pieces of zucchini
1 chunk of yellow bell pepper
2 mini asparagus spears
fresh thyme sprigs
salt and black pepper to taste
basil-infused olive oil

Preheat the oven to 350°F. Soak wooden skewers.

On each skewer, thread a piece of onion on one end and
a mushroom on the other. However you want to arrange the other
vegetables and the fish in the middle is up to you, but after each
piece of fish, tie thyme around the skewer.

When you have loaded up the skewers (they will look very
pretty), season to taste.

Lay them on a baking sheet covered with parchment paper.

Drizzle with the basil-infused olive oil.

Bake for about 15 minutes, turning halfway through the cooking.

Colorful and crunchy—and a healthy fish kabob.

brilliant basmati rice

serves 8

2 tablespoons olive oil
1 onion, peeled and left whole
1⅔ cups basmati rice

2½ cups boiled water
salt to taste

Put the oil in a saucepan and put the onion in the middle.

Gently warm the oil and let the onion disperse its flavors for just a minute—do not let the onion burn.

Put the rice in a strainer and rinse with water until the water runs clear.

Put the rinsed rice into the saucepan that has the onion in. Pour in the boiled water. Season to taste.

Mix together and bring to a boil, then turn the heat to low.

Put a sheet of foil over the saucepan and cover tightly with the lid. Simmer for 30 minutes. Remove from the heat and leave for 10 minutes, with the pan still covered.

Break the onion into the rice.

Check the seasoning before serving.

Rice that is soooo nice!

oy ya broccoli

serves 8

1¾ pounds broccoli florets
2 tablespoons garlic-infused
  olive oil

grated zest of 1 large lemon
squeeze of lemon juice
salt and black pepper to taste

Blanch the broccoli in boiling salted water for a few minutes, so that it is still undercooked. Drain.

Heat the olive oil in a frying pan and fry the broccoli with the lemon zest and juice until crisp-tender, about 1 minute (depending on how you like your broccoli cooked).

Season to taste and serve.

A tasty way of serving broccoli that keeps the freshness and color locked in.

ratatouille princess-style

serves 8–10

6 tablespoons light olive oil
1 red onion, cut into chunks
3 zucchini, about 1¼ pounds
  in total
2 small eggplants, about 1 pound
  in total
2 red bell peppers, sliced
12 small plum or cherry tomatoes,
  about 5 ounces in total

1 tablespoon fresh thyme leaves
⅓ cup chopped parsley
1 garlic clove, crushed
salt and pepper to taste
⅔ cup tomato paste
1 tablespoon sugar

Heat the olive oil in a deep saucepan. Add the chopped onion
and fry until translucent.

Trim the zucchini and cut each into three sections. Slice each
section in half lengthwise, then thinly slice lengthwise
(approximately 2 inches long). Put into the saucepan.

Cut the eggplants into thick slices, then slice again several times.
Add to the zucchini along with the sliced peppers.

Add all the rest of the ingredients to the saucepan.

Put a lid on the saucepan and turn down the heat. Cook for
about 30 minutes, stirring occasionally.

*This wonderful array of colors makes you wish you were in
France, where this dish originates. Ooh la la!*

dark chocolate and limoncello mousse

serves 8

7 ounces bittersweet chocolate
  (70 percent cocoa solids)
1½ tablespoons non-dairy
  margarine (or butter)

4 extra-large eggs, separated
½ cup confectioners' sugar
4 teaspoons limoncello
  (Italian lemon liqueur)

Melt the chocolate in a double-boiler, or in a heatproof bowl set over a saucepan of simmering water. When it has nearly melted, add the margarine and stir until the mixture is smooth.

Remove from the heat and let cool for a few minutes, then carefully add the egg yolks, one at a time.

Beat the egg whites until stiff.

Add the sifted confectioners' sugar to the chocolate mixture.

Fold in the egg whites and then add the limoncello.

Pour into a serving dish or individual coffee cups and refrigerate. Serve chilled.

This soft, velvety chocolate mousse has an amazing, refreshing taste. Limoncello is from Italy; if you can't get it where you live, may I suggest that you hop on a plane and pick up a bottle?

pear tart

serves 8

1 sheet puff pastry, thawed
 if frozen
scant 1 cup prepared pear purée
1 pound firm pears, peeled
 and sliced

2 tablespoons light brown sugar
1 teaspoon ground cinnamon

Preheat the oven to 400°F.

Lay the pastry on a baking sheet lined with parchment paper.
Pinch a ridge all the way around.

Smooth on a thin layer of pear purée.

Place the pear slices on top of the purée. Don't worry about
making it too perfect: rustic is the look wanted here.

Sprinkle with the sugar and cinnamon.

Bake for about 25 minutes.

So easy and looks very St. Tropez: très délicieux!

vegetarian princess, italian-style

minestrone

serves 8

2 onions, diced
1 garlic clove, chopped
3 tablespoons olive oil
2 cups peeled and
  chopped potatoes
6 tomatoes, skinned (drop the
  tomatoes into boiling water and
  leave for a couple of minutes,
  then drain; the skin will peel
  away easily)
½ head of cauliflower, cut into
  small florets
2 zucchini, peeled and chopped

3 celery ribs, chopped
4 carrots, peeled and chopped
7 ounces green beans, trimmed
  and cut in half
4 bay leaves
2 teaspoons herbes de provence
1 sprig of fresh rosemary
1 cup canned cannellini
  beans, drained and rinsed
about 12 cups vegetable stock,
  or enough stock to cover
  the vegetables
salt and black pepper to taste

Fry the onions and garlic in the olive oil until soft.

Add all the rest of the ingredients. Bring to a boil.

Simmer until all the vegetables are soft, about 30 minutes.

Serve with freshly grated Parmesan and crusty bread. One bowl is never enough!

vegetable lasagna

serves 8

for the lasagna
3 onions, diced
2 eggplants, chopped
⅔ cup olive oil
1 tablespoon garlic purée
salt and black pepper to taste
1½ tablespoons butter
8 ounces spinach leaves, washed
1 cup mascarpone cheese

1 cup shredded Cheddar cheese
¼ teaspoon grated nutmeg
10 ounces fresh lasagna sheets

for the topping
2 tablespoons butter
⅓ cup mascarpone cheese
1 cup shredded Cheddar cheese

Fry the onions and eggplants in the olive oil with the garlic purée until soft. Season well.

Add the butter and the spinach and cook until the spinach wilts; this takes less than a minute.

Remove from the heat and stir in the mascarpone, Cheddar, and nutmeg. Check the seasoning of the sauce..

Grease a baking dish (approximately 11 inches square).

Cook the fresh pasta in a big pan of boiling water with a dash of olive oil and some salt until *al dente*, about 2 minutes. Drain the lasagna sheets and lay them on a dish towel.

Spoon a thin layer of sauce over the bottom of the baking dish, then create a layer of pasta. Continue the layering until you have used all the sauce and lasagna, finishing with a layer of lasagna.

Preheat the oven to 350°F.

To make the topping, stir the butter and mascarpone cheese together in a saucepan until melted. Season to taste.

Pour this on top of the lasagna and sprinkle the Cheddar cheese evenly over the top.

Bake until golden, 20–25 minutes.

A lazy lasagna.

melting nutty raspberry meringue cake

serves 8 (or 6 with very big appetites!)

5 egg whites
1½ cups superfine sugar
1 teaspoon vanilla extract
1 cup hazelnuts, bashed to
   resemble bread crumbs

1¼ cups heavy cream
1 pound fresh raspberries
   (about 4 cups)
confectioners' sugar to taste

Preheat the oven to 325°F.

Beat the egg whites until stiff. Slowly beat in the superfine sugar. Fold in the vanilla and hazelnuts.

Line two 10-inch layer cake pans with parchment paper. Divide the meringue mixture between them.

Bake for about 1 hour. Let cool in the turned-off oven.

Whip the cream. Spread the cream and half the raspberries over one meringue layer and place the other meringue layer on top.

Blend the remaining raspberries with confectioners' sugar to make a purée (you decide how sweet you would like it).

To serve, cut into slices and drizzle with the raspberry sauce.

Dedicated to Prince (the singer, NOT hubby!).

morello cherry bake

serves 8

for the pastry
3 tablespoons all-purpose flour
7 tablespoons sugar
½ cup dairy-free margarine
1 teaspoon baking powder

for the filling
2 extra-large eggs
½ cup dairy-free margarine
½ cup sugar
1¾ cups ground almonds
1 teaspoon vanilla extract
2 cans (14–16 ounces each)
    pitted black cherries, drained

Mix together all the ingredients for the pastry. Put about half of it in the freezer. Refrigerate the remaining pastry for 1 hour.

Preheat the oven to 350°F.

Take the pastry from the refrigerator and roll it out to fit the bottom of a greased 9-inch pan with a removable bottom. (Remove the bottom of the pan, place it on the rolled-out pastry, and draw with a sharp knife around it to get the correct shape.)

Combine all the ingredients for the filling, except the cherries. Mix to a smooth paste, then add the cherries. Pour the mixture over the pastry in the pan.

Take the frozen pastry out of the freezer and grate it over the top of the cherry mixture. Bake for 55 minutes.

You will definitely be left wanting More-llo Cherry Bake!

a second helping of yiddish, with expression

We are experiencing a new Yiddish expressionism phrase—I mean phase. It is everywhere, from in the newspapers to on TV. Everybody is at it and you don't have to be a Jewish Princess (or even Jewish) to love it.

Yiddish mixed up with the English language is so commonplace that Yiddish has moved on from the *shtetl* (village) and is now out there in the marketplace. I know myself when a Yiddish word pops out of my mouth: I am suddenly gesticulating, waving my arms, waving my hands, and raising my eyebrows to the ceiling... After all, Yiddish just isn't Yiddish if it isn't accompanied with a little bit of expressionism.

So in the following pages, I have listed a few Yiddish phrases that I hope will give you a *shtick* (laugh). Don't forget, when you try them out: arms up, hands up, shoulders up, eyebrows up!

*****

My mother will *kvell* (be proud) when she tells all her friends that her daughter is The Jewish Princess.

"Shhh: *nisht* in front of the kinder." (Not in front of the children.) Mom, what don't you want us to hear?

My husband is a *gantseh macher* (big shot) at work and a *putz* (idiot) at home.

Please don't tell anyone what I said; you know what *yachnas* (gossips) people are.

Have you seen that handbag? It is such a *metsiah* (bargain): only $200, down from $400. Do you think I should buy two?

If you have nothing nice to say, say *nisht* (nothing).

My therapist said to tell her what is bothering me. Is she *tsedrayt* (mad)?

My husband is such a *dumkop* (dumb head). He suggested I should go out to work! I need that like a *loch in kop* (a hole in the head).

It was *bashayrt* (fate) that I went out with my husband. I stalked him for six months.

I *shlepped* (traveled a long way) everywhere to buy these shoes and now my feet are killing me.

So I asked him, "Does my *tuches* (bottom) look big in these?" He said, "It depends how far away you stand." What *chutzpah* (cheek)!

It is such a *krank* (sickness): She can eat whatever she likes and she still looks like a *langer lockshen* (long and thin).

Don't drive me *meshugga* (mad). Even though I am a Jewish Princess, I can't be a *maiven* (expert) at everything.

He is a *meshuggener* (madman). He thinks he really is a *maiven* (expert) at everything.

He made such a *megillah* (song and dance) about it. It was only the credit card bill!

They have so many *chotchkehs* (small ornaments) in that museum, it must take hours to keep that place *shpigelt* (clean).

My husband is such a *shmuck* (the literal meaning is a penis, but this is often used to mean an idiot). My husband is such a *shmerill* (idiot). My husband is such a *shmendrick* (idiot). But I love him!

You remember him? The *nebbish* (nerd), the *nudnik* (pest), the one that drove me *meshugga* to take me out? He became a brain surgeon.

When you buy heavy items, use your *saychel* (common sense): Always have them delivered!

Oh, stop being so *schmaltzy* (over-the-top lovey-dovey); just hand over the ring!

A *shmear* (enough to butter) of cream cheese, a lot of lox (smoked salmon), a slice of lemon, and a *bissel* (small amount) of black pepper make the perfect bagel.

His salary had a lot of bagels (zeros) after the 1.

A *bissel* (small amount) more cheesecake, please. Are you sure there are only 100 calories in every bite?

She *shlepped naches* (took a lot of pride) when her *boychik* (little boy) had the lead in the school play. He was a tree.

On *shabbos* (Sabbath) after lunch, *Zaydeh* (Grandfather) usually takes a long *shluff* (sleep).

Always on *simchas* (happy occasions). It is said at happy occasions—and also when someone dies.

The salesman gave such a bad *spiel* (patter) that she advised him, "Next time you try telephone sales, stay *shtoom* (quiet)."

Are you sure the deal is kosher (legitimate)?

Oh, that *shmai drai* (knicknack)? It's a Picasso.

Oh, this *shmatta* (piece of cloth)? It's Gucci.

Stop making a *matzo* pudding (a big deal) out of it; I only suggested that we go shopping.

Stop *noodging* (irritating) me. I'll go shopping when I am good and ready!

Oy gevalt! The expression to use for when you are shocked—for example when you put on a pound.

Osa (get real) if you think I am going to do the dishwashing.

The Jewish Princess Feasts & Festivals is full of *chien* (cheeky jokes)!

The recipes in *The Jewish Princess Feasts & Festivals* are a *meichel* for the *beichel* (a gift for the stomach).

Shoyn genug! (That's enough!)

Once a Jewish Princess...

The Jewish Princess gets to the Pearly Gates.

She says, "Leave the bags outside.
I want to check the rooms before I come in."

www.thejewishprincess.com

almond pudding 184
apple
    & pine nut strudel 95
    baked 77
    celery root &, mash 71
    lime &, slaw 74
    sweet potato &, *latkes* 110
    tarte tatin 83
asparagus
    borekas 148
    halibut kabobs 188
    princess pinwheels 161
    sesame sugarsnap &, 182
avocado
    & scallion cream cheese
        125
    filled 179

bagel chips 123
baked apples 77
bananas
    peach & custard cake 82
    breakfast banana loaf 130
bar/bat mitzvah 135–51
beef
    matzo meat parcels 40–1
    roast beef 66
    sweet-and-sour meatballs 92–3
blinis 176
blintzes, cherry-cheese 56–7
blueberry & sour cream sponge
    cake 163
bobbie bagels 33
borekas, asparagus 148
breakfast banana loaf 130
bris brunch 121–33
broccoli, oy ya 190
bubbelehs 34
butternut squash & red onion
    salad 145

cabbage
    challishing holishkas 88–9
    coleslaw 143
    lime & apple slaw 74
cakes
    banana, peach & custard 82

blueberry & sour cream 163
breakfast banana loaf 130
chocolate-sour cream 59
cinnamon 131
ginger-beer 79
holiday fruit 115
honey 81
melting nutty raspberry
    meringue 198
princess *plava* 47
canapés
    blinis 176
    green olive tapenade 175
    handbag sandwich 159
    mini maccabiah balls 108
    pizza straws 177
    princess pinwheels 161
caramel nuts 117
cauliflower with a kick 183
celery root & apple mash 71
challah
    cheaters' doughnuts 112
    pizza 146
challishing holishkas 88–9
Champagne salmon 68–9
cheese
    asparagus *borekas* 148
    avocado & scallion
        cream cheese 125
    challah pizza 146
    cherry-cheese blintzes 56–7
    feta fatter potatoes 107
    mozzarella & onion tart 147
    mushroom bake 149
    princess rarebit 150
    smoked-salmon cream
        cheese 125
    spinach dip 138
    spinach & ricotta tart 52
    strawberry, feta & toasted
        pecan salad 53
    stuffed vegetarian peppers 94
    sun-dried tomato & basil
        cream cheese 124
    tuna & celery cream
        cheese 124
    vegetable lasagna 196–7

cheesecake, Mars bar 60–1
cherries
    cheese blintzes 56–7
    chocolate-cherry fudge 113
    morello cherry bake 199
chickpeas, hummus 139
chicken
    marmalade 70
    princess tahini-fried 109
    rosemary & lemon 42
    a *shissel* of *shikerer* 22
    Spanish 65
    stuffed chicken thighs 180
chocolate
    & cherry fudge 113
    duo-oh-oh-oh! 58
    sour cream cake 59
    coconutties 44
    florentines 164–5
    hot chocolate pudding 116
    & limoncello mousse 192
    Mars bar cheesecake 60–1
    pear &, crisp 96–7
    & prune hamantaschen 24–5
    rugelach 132–3
    truffles 114
cinnamon baubles 43
cinnamon cake 131
clementines in caramel 185
coconut rice pudding 55
coconutties 44
coleslaw 143
cookies
    honey 80
    kosher wine *kichels* 162
    muesli breakfast cookies 129
    "must-have" macaroons 46
    strudel 100–1
    triple chocolate chip 167
corn fritters 106
crisp, pear & chocolate 96–7

dinner parties 171–99
dips
    avocado & scallion
        cream cheese 125
    hummus 139

smoked-salmon cream
   cheese 125
spinach 138
sun-dried tomato & basil
   cream cheese 124
tuna & celery cream
   cheese 124
doughnuts, cheaters' 112
drunken fish 21

eggplant
   easy pâté 140
   matzo meat parcels 40–1
   stuffed vegetarian peppers 94
   ratatouille, princess-style 191
   vegetable lasagna 196–7
eggs
   loaded avocados 179
   matzo *brie* 35
   princess rarebit 150
   shakshuka 128
   tortilla, princess-style 126–7
   triple deckers 160

feta fatter potatoes 107
feta, strawberry & toasted
   pecan salad 53
fish
   Champagne salmon 68–9
   drunken fish 21
   gefilte 37–9
   halibut kabobs 188
   handbag sandwich 159
   princess potato salad 76
   smoked-salmon cream
      cheese 125
   tuna & celery cream
      cheese 124
florentines 164–5
fritlach 26
fritters, corn 106
fruit
   banana, peach & custard
      cake 82
   blueberry & sour cream
      sponge cake 163
   cherry-cheese blintzes 56–7

melon, pomegranate &
   ginger salad 78
melting nutty raspberry
   meringue cake 198
morello cherry bake 199
pear & chocolate crisp
   96–7
pear Waldorf salad 141
perfect peach kuchen 98–9
posh pears 27
strawberry, feta & toasted
   pecan salad 53
tarte tatin 83
fudge, chocolate-cherry 113

gefilte fish 37–9
ginger-beer cake 79
grandma's matzo pudding 45
granola, princess Passover 36
green beans & mushrooms 72
green olive tapenade 175

halibut kabobs 188
hamantaschen, prune &
   chocolate 24–5
handbag sandwich 159
Hanukkah 103–17
holiday fruit cake 115
honey cookies 80
honey cake 81
hot chocolate pudding 116
hummus 139

Israeli salad 73

jerk burgers 23

kabobs, halibut 188
kosher wine *kichels* 162
kuchen, perfect peach 98–9
kugel, princess-perfect potato 75
lamb
   challishing holishkas 88–9
   lemon-chile chops 91
   tagine 90
latkes, sweet potato & apple 110
lemon-chile chops 91

lemon & rosemary chicken 42
lime & apple slaw 74

macaroons, "must-have" 46
maccabiah balls, mini 108
Mars bar cheesecake 60–1
matzo
   brie 35
   grandma's pudding 45
   meat parcels 40–1
   princess Passover granola 36
meatballs, sweet-and-sour 92–3
melon, pomegranate & ginger
   salad 78
minestrone 195
morello cherry bake 199
mozzarella & onion tart 147
muesli breakfast cookies 129
mushroom(s)
   bake 149
   green beans & 72
   halibut kabobs 188
   soup 187
   stuffed chicken thighs 180
   stuffed vegetarian peppers 94
   vegetable risotto 54

noo potatoes! 181
noodle & edamame salad 142

olives
   green, tapenade 175
   pizza straws 177
onions
   mozzarella &, tart 147
   roasted butternut squash &
      red onion salad 145
oy ya broccoli 190

pancakes, Passover 34
Passover 29–47
pasta
   mushroom bake 149
   vegetable lasagna 196–7
pâté, eggplant 140
peach
   banana & custard cake 82

perfect kuchen 98–9
pear(s)
  & chocolate crisp 96–7
  tart 193
  Waldorf salad 141
  posh 27
peppers (bell), princess stuffed
  vegetarian 94
perfect peach kuchen 98–9
pine nut & apple strudel 95
pinwheels, princess 161
pizza
  challah 146
  straws 177
plava, princess 47
posh pears 27
potatoes
  feta fatter 107
  lyonnaise 50
  matzo meat parcels 40–1
  mini maccabiah balls 108
  noo potatoes! 181
  princess-perfect *kugel* 75
  princess potato salad 76
  tortilla, princess-style 126–7
prune & chocolate
  hamantaschen 24–5
pudding
  almond 184
  coconut rice 55
  grandma's matzo 45
  hot chocolate 116
Purim 19–27

rarebit, princess 150
ratatouille, princess-style 191
rice
  brilliant basmati 189
  challishing holishkas 88–9
  coconut rice pudding 55
  stuffed vegetarian peppers 94
  vegetable risotto 54
roast beef 66
roasted butternut squash & red
  onion salad 145
rosemary & lemon chicken 42
Rosh Hashanah 63–83

rugelach, chocolate 132–3

salads
  coleslaw 143
  edamame & noodle 142
  Israeli 73
  lime & apple slaw 74
  pear Waldorf 141
  princess potato 76
  roasted butternut squash & red
    onion 145
  strawberry, feta & toasted
    pecan 53
  sugarsnap peas, spinach
    & chile 144
salmon
  Champagne 68–9
  handbag sandwich 159
  princess potato salad 76
  smoked cream cheese 125
sandwiches 158
  handbag 159
  triple deckers 160
scones, princess 166
sesame sugarsnap &
  asparagus crunch 182
shakshuka 128
Shavuot 49–61
a *shissel* of *shikerer* chicken 22
soup
  minestrone 195
  mushroom 187
Spanish chicken 65
spinach
  dip 138
  princess 51
  & ricotta tart 52
  sugarsnap peas, chile &,
    salad 144
  vegetable lasagna 196–7
  strawberry, feta & toasted
    pecan salad 53
strudel, apple and pine nut 95
strudel cookies 100–1
Succot 85–101
sweet potatoes
  lamb tagine 90

princess-perfect potato *kugel* 75
  & apple *latkes* 110
sweet-and-sour meatballs 92–3

tagine, lamb 90
tahini-fried chicken 109
tapenade, green olive 175
tarte tatin 83
tarts (savory)
  mozzarella & onion 147
  spinach & ricotta 52
tomatoes
  minestrone 195
  noo potatoes! 181
  pizza straws 177
  princess rarebit 150
  ratatouille princess-style 191
  shakshuka 128
  stuffed chicken thighs 180
  sun-dried & basil cream
    cheese 124
  sweet-and-sour meatballs 92–3
  triple deckers 160
tortilla, princess-style 126–7
triple chocolate chip cookies
  167
triple deckers 160
truffles, chocolate 114
tuna & celery cream cheese 124
turkey
  jerk burgers 23

vegetable lasagna 196–7
vegetable risotto 54
vegetarian dishes
  minestrone 195
  stuffed peppers 94

Waldorf salad, pear 141
weddings 153–67

Yom Kippur 63–4
Yorkshire puddings 67

zucchini
  ratatouille princess-style 191
  zucchini, Italian-style 111